Evaluating Teachers
and Administrators

Other Titles in This Series

Education in Rural America: A Reassessment of Conventional Wisdom, edited by Jonathan Sher

Westview Special Studies in Education

Evaluating Teachers and Administrators:
A Performance Objectives Approach
George B. Redfern

Stressing the importance of using evaluation as a means to improve teacher and administrator performance, Dr. Redfern provides a practical guide to conducting an evaluation and using its results. He thoroughly describes the anatomy of the evaluation process, outlines the materials needed, and covers such often-neglected topics as evaluation of substandard performance, assessment of the performance of administrators and supervisors, evaluation as an administrative tool in education management, and the potential pitfalls inherent in the evaluation process. The book closes with detailed suggestions for developing or revising programs for personnel evaluation.

George B. Redfern, now an education management consultant, formerly served as executive vice-president of the Institute for Leadership Achievement, deputy executive secretary of the American Association of School Administrators, and as a principal in the Ohio public school system.

Evaluating Teachers and Administrators: A Performance Objectives Approach

George B. Redfern

Westview Press / Boulder, Colorado

Westview Special Studies in Education

Copyright © 1980 by Westview Press, Inc.

Published in 1980 in the United States of America by
    Westview Press, Inc.
    5500 Central Avenue
    Boulder, Colorado 80301
    Frederick A. Praeger, Publisher

Library of Congress Cataloging in Publication Data
Redfern, George B.
    Evaluating teachers and administrators.
    (Westview special studies in education)
    Bibliography: p.
    Includes index.
    1. School administrators, Rating of. 2. Teachers, Rating of. I. Title.
LB2831.66.R42   371.1'44   79-23966
ISBN 0-89158-760-8
ISBN 0-89158-890-6 pbk.

Printed and bound in the United States of America

Contents

Figures, Tables, and Forms

Preface

The author's quest for a more effective way to evaluate the performance of teachers and administrators has covered a long period and has followed varied pathways. An extended period of service in school personnel management and general administration in the Cincinnati Public Schools provided many opportunities to test the operational feasibility and practicality of evolving evaluation techniques. The move from quite conventional toward more imaginative procedures was a slow but steady process. During this period of time, many teachers, principals, and central-office specialists contributed greatly by helping in many ways to provide a laboratory to try out concepts and procedures.

A broader scope of opportunity emerged during the nine years the author served on the staff of the American Association of School Administrators (AASA). These years made possible the chance to extend the quest beyond the boundaries of one large school system and to engage in a nationwide effort to promote better ways to evaluate personnel performance. While a member of the staff of AASA, it was possible to serve as a professor for its National Academy for School Executives in numerous seminars and other in-service activities. These opportunities made it possible to advocate a particular point of view about evaluation that put the emphasis upon using the process as a means to promote improvement in performance, rather than just to provide a postperformance "report card" as so many traditional assessment procedures do.

After retiring as deputy executive secretary of AASA, a new

kind of opportunity became possible. The chance to work on a nationwide basis as a consultant for many individual school systems made it possible once again to directly assist teachers, administrators, and supervisors in the design of new programs or in the restructuring of existing plans of evaluation of personnel performance. As a consultant, the author was not only able to help prepare school systems to design and develop more meaningful assessment programs, but also to remain with the school systems over a sufficient period of time to help install the programs and later to audit their effectiveness. These opportunities made it possible for many teaching, administrative, and supervisory people to contribute to the techniques and the ideas with which this volume is concerned.

During these years, it was possible also to participate in a wide variety of activities sponsored by the School Management Institute, Inc. (SMI), of Ohio. Through its many in-service and staff development programs, the search for more useful and productive approaches in evaluation could be continued. SMI also made it possible to produce, publish, and distribute publications, audiovisual materials, and other training aids on the subject of evaluation.

These experiences, confirmed by many others in education, government, and industry, have shown that the in-service training of teachers, administrators, and supervisors has been underemphasized and inadequate. It is relatively easy to generate an initial sense of excitement and enthusiasm for newer approaches to evaluation, only to see it falter and fade away simply because of a lack of follow-through and an inadequate emphasis upon concepts and skills in ongoing staff development programs.

To contribute to better staff development programs in the evaluation of teaching, three volumes (all published by SMI) have preceded this one. In 1963, *How to Appraise Teaching Performance* was published. In 1972, that volume was replaced by *How to Evaluate Teaching: A Performance Objectives Approach.* A third book, *Evaluating Teachers and Administrators: Putting the Pieces Together,* was issued in 1977. Now, this revision of the 1972 publication brings up to date the continuing effort to promote the performance objectives point of view for the evaluation of teachers and administrators.

During the years, countless persons have contributed to this continuing effort. It would be impossible to name and describe the specific contributions of each, yet to all of them—though nameless—grateful appreciation is extended.

A word about the need for a genderless pronoun: the masculine is used throughout, but it is used with the understanding that it represents, semantically and intentionally, the feminine gender as well.

G.B.R.

Evaluating Teachers
and Administrators

Introduction

The essential elements of a useful program of personnel evaluation depend, to a large extent, upon the points of view of those who design the evaluation procedures. Circumstances and factors in school systems also influence the focus and form of evaluation programs. The designers of a program ideally may desire to establish procedures that fulfill the goals of improvement in performance and professional development, but they may be obliged to settle for less because of seemingly insurmountable constraints indigenous to the situation.

Improvement in performance is widely acclaimed as a most desirable goal of personnel evaluation; yet the types and kinds of evaluation procedures developed often make the attainment of this goal very difficult. For whatever reasons, many evaluation programs stress postperformance ratings that depend largely upon assessments of a superior-subordinate nature.

It is important that the designers of the evaluation procedures consider realistically the kind of program they can design and recommend. If improved performance and professional development are to be the principal goals, the elements of the program must be compatible with and contribute to those goals.

As conceived in this publication, the most useful personnel evaluation program will

1. engender cooperative effort between the person being appraised and the one(s) doing the evaluating;
2. foster good communication between (or among) the parties;

3. put premiums on identifying what needs improving, planning how to achieve the needed improvements, and determining how the results will be evaluated;
4. promote professional growth and development of the person being appraised;
5. stress the importance of evaluators becoming insightful and skilled in the art of evaluating; and
6. make a commitment to the proposition that the bottom line is greater effectiveness in the teaching/learning/supervising process.

The prerequisite of any good evaluation program is a clear and comprehensive definition of the duties and responsibilities of each position. It is vital that the expectations for all positions be spelled out in detail so that those involved (evaluatees as well as evaluators) know what they are.

The initial step in evaluation is the identification of matters on which emphasis should be placed to enable the individual to be more effective as a result of the evaluation. Diagnosis of these needs is an endeavor shared by both the person being appraised and the evaluator, but ideas and suggestions can also come from clients. (For teaching personnel, clients can be students and parents; for administrators, they can be teachers and other employees.) Circumstances will dictate whether input from client sources is practical and feasible.

Once needs are identified, it becomes possible to decide how best to respond to them. Response options range from informal, unstructured endeavors to the forming of very specific performance objectives and plans of action to attain them. The implementation of a plan of action takes place during the span of time in which evaluation occurs and consists of the interactions between those involved in the process. Included are observations, feedback, interim and checkup conferences.

The assessment of results is also a cooperative endeavor. Generally, both the evaluatee and the evaluator assess the extent to which specific projects have been completed or objectives have been attained. Effectiveness of overall performance in major areas of responsibility is assessed by the evaluator. The process culminates with a conference between the evaluatee and the evaluator to discuss the implications of the results and to plan further action.

The above is an overview of a promising approach to personnel evaluation that is a productive and realistic way to establish a results-oriented evaluation program. Successful teaching and administration do not come about by accident. Able persons plan, implement their plans, and, it is hoped, evaluate the results of those plans. This is the essence of evaluation by objectives. First, then, intelligent, well-prepared, resourceful teachers and administrators are essential in the delivery of effective educational services. Second, a clear understanding of the expectations for assignments is required. The roles of administrators and supervisors must be clarified, and a familiarity with the criteria upon which success or failure will be judged is a must. A plan for fulfilling goals and objectives must be designed and carried out. Assessments should be made on the basis of results, and the implications of these need to be discussed by the individual and his evaluator. These components, fitted together in a coherent manner, constitute a sound evaluation program.

The evaluation of personnel performance has baffled teachers and school administrators for many years. Much of the difficulty stems from an uncertainty about the focal point of assessment: Should the focus be on the individual as a person or on the results of his efforts? The two are intertwined, but the evaluation process is pointless unless the starting point is to determine the effectiveness of the results.

Other difficulties arise when the purpose of the evaluation process is unclear or when the process is nothing more than an inspection for rating purposes. What a rater elects to observe and rate often is unacceptable to the person being observed. Evaluators may not be skilled and perceptive in making observations and judgments may be inconclusive and superficial. In fact, observation as a major method of measuring success on the job often is of doubtful validity.

Differentials in pay, based upon evaluations of teachers and administrators, further complicate evaluation. Weighing the relative merits of a total staff to recommend variations in compensation is neither simple nor readily acceptable to those being evaluated or even to those doing the evaluating. The greatest problem has been an inability to devise a sound process of evaluation.

When the purpose of evaluation becomes the improvement of performance instead of merely the rating of it, results are more productive. Most people want to work more effectively. The stimulation of growth and development is a goal that is more acceptable to teachers and administrators than simply getting a report card indicating an evaluator's judgment of the individual's performance. Creativity and teamwork replace the uncertainty, misunderstanding, and purposelessness that frequently are associated with evaluation programs based solely on rating.

Evaluation practices vary widely among school districts. The predominant one is a process of formalized rating, despite the dissatisfactions of those who are obliged to carry out the process. Small districts often show more initiative and inclination to devise and administer successful programs than large districts. Seldom do two school systems have identical evaluation procedures, although similarities may exist.

Because of perfunctory rating, the goal of evaluation is often obscure, but the goal should be to enable an individual to do a better job. To deliver improved educational services for children should be the objective as seen by the individual and the evalutor. They have a joint responsibility to make an individual's performance contribute as much as possible to the level of performance of one grade or the entire school. But improved performance is achieved in several ways: self-endeavor, helpful supervision, a stimulating learning environment, optimum quantities of learning materials and supplies, and a supportive climate. Systematic evaluation is only one means of stimulating improvement.

It is well, however, to remember the inadvisability of expecting that a composite design of evaluation will satisfy every human need and all the requirements of all school systems. Variations in the size and complexity of school systems, different leadership styles of principals and supervisors, and the varying needs of individual teachers require flexibility in applying evaluation procedures.

The impetus for instituting or revising an evaluation program should come from the highest level; the superintendent and board of education must believe in and support the idea. In fact, the board of education must do more than just believe in having a good evaluation program. It must understand fully what is involved and be willing to give the program status and support, which includes authorizing financial support as needed to develop and carry out the program.

Accountability requires that individuals know clearly what is expected of them. It means having access to the ways and means of attaining performance expectations and involves a relevant assessment of the results achieved. The evaluation component in an accountability program parallels the steps in performance objectives evaluation for teachers and administrators. In both instances, the typical sequence involves identifying needs, considering options and activities, determining objectives and action plans, monitoring progress, providing assistance, making summative assessments of results, and discussing the implications of the outcomes.

1
The Performance Objectives Approach

Why is it that successful evaluation procedures are difficult to achieve even though interest in evaluation is high? Some school systems have gained recognition for the success they have had in making evaluation work; others have experienced only nominal success.

The case for having an effective program of evaluation is easy to make. Obviously individuals vary widely in the quantity and quality of their services. The able, despite very marked gains in compensation, are usually underpaid; the less able probably are overcompensated. Many, in a nonmaterial sense, are more worthy of recognition than others. The need for an effective evaluation program is one thing; finding the means to achieve workable procedures is another. The crux of the problem lies in the development of techniques that will be satisfactory and acceptable, both to the individual being evaluated and to those responsible for the evaluating.

It is logical to assume that individuals have inherent competencies that can be identified and described. These competencies may be expressed in terms of techniques in carrying out the teaching/learning process and the attainment of measurable learner outcomes. If performance competencies can be identified, appraisal procedures can be designed to ascertain the extent to which an individual demonstrates such competencies. An evaluator looks primarily for results rather than for evidence of any effort to change behavior. Does it make sense to require regular assessments of professional performance? A quick answer is, yes, it makes good sense. Since improvement in performance is the name of the game, evaluation should be a means to bring this about. It is presumed that most people do desire to improve; it is further assumed that the able as well as the less able can find some area or skill that needs improvement.

The possibilities for improvement are greater if evaluation is a regular, required process (provided planning of the evaluation process is carefully done), follow-through is conscientious and consistent, and results are forthrightly assessed. Evaluation by objectives is best achieved when evaluatee and evaluator jointly establish work objectives, agree upon well-established action plans, and measure accomplishment in terms of outcomes and results attained.

Required evaluation may generate some apprehension on the part of evaluatees and their evaluators. Some discontent can be good because it may cause a school system to seek reasons for expressed or implied dissatisfaction. In so doing, inadequate evaluation procedures may be identified and replaced.

Unfortunately, too many people have unrealistic and unwarranted expectations as to what a sound program of evaluation can accomplish. Some want to use it to get rid of deadwood. Others want it to be precise enough to institute differentials in compensation. Still others see it as a means of guaranteeing accountability. Some want to give the appearance of having an effective program of evaluation when the procedures are not really very productive. Almost all verbalize the prime reason for evaluation as the improvement of performance. To expect most traditional programs of evaluation to accomplish all these aims is nonsense.

Evaluation actually should be regarded as a diagnostic process, enabling individuals and their evaluators to focus on appropriate objectives—objectives that, if accomplished, will produce better and more effective services. Evaluation is a means, not an end. It can and should produce feedback that can be used to alter performance techniques and strategies.

It is probable that most administrators are less than enthusiastic about serving as evaluators for teachers and other personnel. This is due, in part, to the nature of the evaluator's role in most current evaluation programs. Too much is judgmental in conventional evaluation programs. Principals and other evaluators have to "lay it on the line" without enough data to justify their opinions. They often lack technical skills in evaluation. They may feel certain inadequacies in the evaluatee's area of specialization. It is not easy or pleasant to hold an evaluation review conference if the individual's performance has been marginal or unsatisfactory. Some administrators are also afflicted with inflated egos, which makes evaluatee-evaluator interaction more of a confrontation than a useful function.

Given certain preconceived notions about conventional evaluation procedures, administrators may view with varying degrees of trepidation the trend toward a greater emphasis upon evaluation to achieve measurable results by means of specific objectives. There is no doubt that evaluation by objectives puts new demands upon the leadership talents of school administrators who are involved in the process. They are obliged to know more about evaluation as a process. They have to improve their skills in helping teachers set appropriate performance objectives. They are obliged to devise better monitoring and information-gathering techniques. And, inescapably, they have to perfect counseling and conference competencies.

Probably the most significant new demand is the need to allocate more time for supervision and evaluation. Perhaps as much as 40 percent of leadership time must be devoted to these activities. Given the current inordinate amount of time needed for administrative tasks, crisis resolution, public and community relations, and purely managerial duties, most administrators are likely to reply that there is just no way to reallocate time priorities to increase the emphasis upon supervision and evaluation.

How, then, can this obvious dilemma be resolved? An equally obvious solution is to make some hard decisions about the following questions.

1. What is the primary emphasis in a principal's job—instructional leadership or managerial details?
2. How can supervisory personnel and instructional specialists become more substantively involved in the evaluation process? Or should they?
3. How much can and should school systems invest in in-

service development to enable administrators and supervisors to develop a better conception of evaluation and to
perfect skills in its implementation?

4. How can administrators be helped to see evaluation as an affirmative opportunity rather than a negative encumbrance?

5. How can board of education members be encouraged to
view evaluation less as a tool to terminate personnel and
more as a process to improve performance? (Top-level
perception and viewpoint are crucial to the success of
newer approaches to evaluation.)

These are the key questions that leadership personnel must
grapple with if evaluation is to change from being a primarily
pedestrian process to one that is challenging and potentially
productive. It is to be hoped, therefore, that the attitude of
administrators toward newer approaches to evaluation will be
a receptive one and that they will elevate this important enterprise to a higher level of priority.

Teachers and administrators view evaluation with mixed
emotions. Some are unalterably hostile to it; others are dis-
illusioned with existing practices; many feel uncertain, and
often threatened, about rating procedures that are administra-
tively conceived, designed, and implemented. They doubt that
such evaluation processes are in their best interests or stimulate
improvement. They are likely to feel that, at best, rating is a
neutral process and that, at worst, it is probably detrimental to
the individual's welfare, especially if its primary purpose is to
categorize competencies into scaled classifications.

However, if teachers and other staff members are partners
with administrators and supervisors in all phases of evaluation,
attitudes can be quite different. Evaluation by objectives is a
partnership process. This is one of its prime assets. Evaluatees
are in on the ground floor when modifications of existing programs of evaluation are being considered or new programs of
evaluation are being developed.

Some Results of a Performance Objectives Approach

What are some of the results that may logically be expected
from a performance objectives approach to evaluation?

Clearer Perceptions of Performance Expectations

The process definitely clarifies the scope of an individual's duties and responsibilities. This comes about especially during the needs assessment process conducted before specific performance objectives are determined. When both the evaluatee and the evaluator survey all of the former's job requirements, both parties are given the opportunity to see more clearly the total spectrum of performance expectations. Unless a person understands what is expected of him, it is difficult to see how he can wisely determine where efforts should be concentrated to bring about both qualitative and quantitative improvement in performance.

Use of Feedback to Refine Performance Strategies and Procedures

Evaluatees profit most when information regarding their performance is communicated to them in a timely manner. Feedback needs to be used as it becomes available. Periodic progress evaluations, throughout the year, should be used to modify performance procedures, to alter objectives, to discard some, and to replace those discarded with more relevant ones.

Availability of More Valid Performance Data

The major emphasis in this type of evaluation is upon collecting, analyzing, and assessing performance information. These data enable both the evaluatee and the evaluator to be more precise in making judgments about and estimates of accomplishment. The more data available, the more valid the assessments will be. The difficulty in most traditional rating procedures is that judgments are made upon insufficient data. Performance objectives programs of evaluation reverse this tendency.

Reinforced Practitioner-Supervisor Relationships

The performance objectives approach to evaluation changes the nature of the working relations between practitioner and supervisor as the emphasis is upon a partnership. Furthermore, the hesitancy that supervisors generally exhibit toward getting actively involved in a rating type of evaluation program can be removed because the purpose of the process is different. Educational umpiring, so disliked by supervisors, is not required. In fact, evaluation and supervision, in the context being considered, are compatible. One complements the other, and both have the same purpose: to improve performance.

Greater Sensitivity to Needs and Concerns of Clients

It is repeatedly emphasized that, in evaluation by objectives, a major consideration is the learning achievements of students. The welfare of the student/client is paramount. Performance objectives stress what happens to students under the instruction and guidance of the teacher. While objectives may be fixed in other areas, the learners' needs and concerns come first.

Stronger Emphasis upon Improvement

Greater practitioner proficiency is the focus of the evaluation process. While other purposes may be included, they are secondary to the central purpose of improvement. It is in the best interests of the individual being evaluated, the students served, and the school system's program to put the emphasis upon performance improvement. It makes evaluation a positive rather than a negative process.

More Adequate Documentation of Extent of Incompetency

While the major emphasis is upon improvement, it is not possible to avoid the necessity, on occasion, to document areas of inadequacy or incompetency. Inasmuch as performance objectives evaluation stresses the importance of an early specification of deficiencies in performance, plus careful and adequate administrative and supervisory assistance to help the individual overcome deficiencies, it is possible to do a more thorough job of documenting the whole procedure. Carefully kept records of help provided, data monitored, and results achieved become the documentation that is necessary if and when due process must be carried out.

Skill in Evaluation Requires Higher Priority

Skill in evaluation is not often given a high enough priority on the list of administrative and supervisory responsibilities by principals and other administrators. Educational administration courses underemphasize it. School systems rarely make skill in evaluation a requirement for appointment to a leadership post, and it is usually not stressed in staff development programs for administrators and supervisors after they assume their positions. Yet evaluator skills are tremendously important in performance objectives evaluation, and, as administrators see the need more clearly, they will accommodate themselves to a realignment of their job priorities.

* * *

Performance objectives evaluation offers opportunities for the improvement of individuals and the product of their efforts. The question is, What will educators do with these opportunities? If they take advantage of them to design promising new approaches to the evaluation process, they stand to reap many benefits. If they merely retread obsolete procedures by means of patchwork and cosmetic applications, they will have passed up golden opportunities.

An Evaluation Model

While it is difficult to prescribe an evaluation model that may be appropriate for all school systems, there are common elements that have wide applicability. There are six basic components that are essential in a performance objectives–oriented program aimed at improving an individual's performance (see Figure 1.1). A brief description of each step is given here, and detailed explanations are provided in subsequent chapters.

Responsibility Criteria

Duties and responsibilities required in the performance of an assignment must be indicated. Most school systems have developed criteria of one sort or another that can be used for evaluating performance. (Specific sets of criteria are listed in chapters 2 and 4.)

Identify Needs

Using responsibility criteria, the evaluatee and the evaluator cooperatively identify the status of the former's current per-

Figure 1.1

Evaluation Model

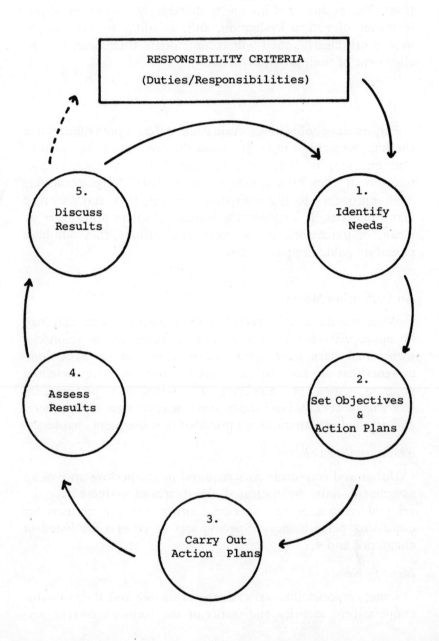

formance. The identification of current strengths and areas of difficulty can be useful in deciding the kinds and number of specific objectives and action plans to establish.

Set Objectives and Action Plans

Objectives and action plans are the means to achieve desired outcomes determined by the evaluation process. Several questions arise as objectives are being formulated. How will they be stated? In behavioral terms? Or in terms of learner achievement? Or both? Will the attempt be to effect a change of behavior on the part of the teacher or the pupil? Or both? If learner achievement is the consideration, will the performance objectives be directed toward gains in both the cognitive and the affective domains? (The former are easier to design and to measure than the latter.) The art of drafting objectives must be cultivated.

At the time performance objectives are agreed upon, it is important to discuss the actions and efforts that will be expended to attain the objectives. If the objectives concentrate upon changes in the behavior of the evaluatee, what types of changes will these be? Alterations in teaching or administrative style and tactics? Better planning? Greater flexibility and adjustability? Increased emphasis upon innovation and creativity? More realistic evaluation of pupil achievement? If these are to be objectives, both the evaluatee and the evaluator must plan actions and activities calculated to bring about the desired changes in teacher behavior.

If the performance objectives include achievement gains of the learner, the emphasis will be upon actions to bring about such gains. The evaluatee and evaluator will decide what instructional and administrative procedures will be employed. There will be a concentration upon a better grasp of concepts and an emphasis upon skill development. The evaluatee and the evaluator pursue these actions cooperatively. Both have a vested interest in the outcome.

Carry Out Action Plans

Traditionally, monitoring and evaluating have been done simultaneously, and observation of teaching performance has been essentially an evaluative process. Little, if any, effort has been made to distinguish between monitoring and evaluation. It has been like deciding the winner of a game long before it has ended.

The evaluator should monitor the evaluatee's performance to collect data and information that relate to the objectives being pursued. Monitoring is concerned with performance outputs; it is the evidence-gathering part of the total evaluation process. The parties involved must discuss and, it is to be hoped, agree upon certain matters concerning the monitoring (i.e., the data-gathering forms to be used, kinds and frequency of visitations, identity of monitors, and the use of any mechanical monitors, conferences, and other types of contacts). A substantial volume of appropriate information enhances good evaluation and may also result in immediate change for improvement. Information from the monitoring should never be simply stored away when prompt feedback will enhance performance.

Assess Results

Interpreting the meaning and significance of monitored data is a very important part of the total process of evaluation. This represents the culmination of all that has gone before. Goal setting, the determination of objectives, and performance activities all lead up to the evaluation stage.

Evaluation of data is a twofold process. Self-assessment is one part; the evaluator's assessments compose the other. If more than one evaluator is involved, assessment can become a three-part or even a collegial process. Some students of the teacher evaluation process are coming to believe that assessment can and should be a collegial process. Most performance requires primary and secondary evaluators, but various forms of collegial assessment may be used on an experimental basis.

The classic one-on-one, evaluator-evaluatee type of assessment is not very realistic in a large school where there may be dozens of teachers, one principal, and little other administrative or supervisory staff. Also, if the cycle of evaluation periods must begin and end for all teachers at the same time, utilizing a single evaluator is unrealistic when the evaluator-evaluatee ratio is high.

What are the options in the involvement of others in the assessment of monitored data? One possibility is to use a supervisor or consultant to aid the principal in a review of the monitored data. In some secondary schools, the department heads also assess monitored data. Another pattern that has been suggested would involve creating a committee of teachers to assist in the review.

There is mounting interest in having students contribute to the assessment process. In some instances, this has taken the form of student demands; in others, educators have resolved to find better ways to involve the students. Also, in some school systems there are demands that parents should have some role in evaluating the services of teachers and administrators. Obviously the demands for broad participation make a performance-oriented evaluation program essential if the abuses and errors of mass involvement in subjective determinations are to be avoided.

Discuss Results

The evaluation conference is exceedingly important. It is the occasion for the persons most intimately involved in the process to discuss the outcome of their efforts to achieve the objectives. A very important responsibility is placed upon the evaluator to help the evaluatee view evaluation as a constructive rather than a negative process.

There is no set recipe for conducting a productive evaluation conference. Preparation will help. Training is obligatory. If both parties have tried to the fullest to achieve the performance objectives, that fact will contribute to the success of the conference. The most valuable asset, however, is experience on the part of the evaluator.

The evaluation conference will yield ideas for follow-up action. It may develop, during the conference, that the evaluatee will see the need for certain kinds of follow-up activities to reinforce gains already made. The tentative formulation of objectives for the next round of evaluation often takes place during the conference.

Performance objectives evaluation can be the means of enabling individuals to achieve goals that will contribute to improved performance. It is a tool to help people become more competent

in the performance of their duties and responsibilities. Those
duties and responsibilities must continually be evaluated in relationship to the primary task of any school—that of improving
learning opportunities for the students. Evaluation is a worthwhile enterprise and deserves more penetrating and continued
study.

2

Components and Tools of Evaluation

There are a number of components in an evaluation program based upon performance of objectives. Each step in the process is of great importance, and everyone connected with such an evaluation program should have a clear understanding of the importance and procedures of each. The components are discussed generally in this chapter; in succeeding chapters, each will be discussed in further detail in relation to different groups of people or types of performance to be evaluated.

The tools, or materials and forms that may be used, should be kept as simple as possible in a good performance evaluation program. On the other hand, it is advisable to have good records and complete evaluation forms if the final evaluative judgments are to be properly recorded and made a part of an evaluatee's personnel record.

It is quite difficult to prescribe specific forms that can be adopted without modification by all school systems. Instead, it is better for each school system to develop its own forms and records so that they will meet the specifications of the plan adopted. The forms and records suggested here are to be regarded as illustrative only; it is hoped that they may serve as guides for the development of more appropriate ones in the individual school systems that undertake a performance evaluation program.

A common difficulty in the establishment of evaluation plans appears to be a feeling that the forms themselves are the essence of the process. This is not true. Forms and records are merely the tools of evaluation, and planners should not become so preoccupied with form design that they lose sight of the importance of the total process.

Responsibility Criteria

The first component in the evaluation process is a definition of the content and scope of the job. It seems so obvious that a clear understanding of the duties and responsibilities of a job is necessary to the successful completion of the evaluation process. An awareness of job expectations is absolutely essential.

But it is often assumed that once persons are appointed to their positions, they will be able to function with minimal direction and clarification of what is expected of them. Such an assumption is not likely to be correct. It cannot be overemphasized that job understanding should not be left to chance, and a greater emphasis upon job definition is essential. This need not be limited to written job descriptions, although they may be useful. It is likely that a more helpful method of defining the job will be to draw up a list of responsibility criteria (duties/responsibilities), a sample of which for teachers is provided in Form A (sample responsibility criteria for administrators are provided in Form E in Chapter 4).

Teachers and administrators need to be clear about their duties and responsibilities, as do their evaluators. If responsibility criteria are used, it is important to be sure that they are used properly. The criteria are expressed in terms of broad areas with descriptors under each. The latter are provided to clarify the content of each major area; they should not be used as a glorified checklist. The descriptors' primary purpose is to enable both the evaluatee and the evaluator to be clear about the content of each area. The criteria are cast in broad terms in order to have the widest possible applicability to all classifications of teachers or administrators. For those who hold specialized positions, it will be necessary to use their job descriptions as supplementary means to clarify job content.

It will be noted that major areas in the criteria are numbered 100, 200, 300, etc., and descriptors under each are also numbered—101, 102, 103, etc. The reason for using such a numbering system is to facilitate the use of the criteria, especially when identifying needs in the evaluation process.

FORM A

RESPONSIBILITY CRITERIA
(Teachers)

100 - Planning and Organizing

101 - Makes short- and long-range plans
102 - Correlates individual objectives with school and district goals
103 - Adheres to principles of growth and development in planning
104 - Plans appropriate sequence of skills
105 - Has an ongoing program to diagnose and assess needs and progress of individual students
106 - Plans for individual differences
107 - Involves students in planning
108 - Encourages student leadership and participation in decision making
109 - Adjusts physical environment to accommodate variety in learning situations
110 - Cooperates with others in planning daily schedule
111 - Manages time efficiently
112 - Organizes well
113 - Keeps accurate records
114 - Is attentive to conditions that affect the health and safety of students
115 - Organizes work so that substitute teachers can function with a minimum of loss of learning for students
116 - Other (specify)

200 - Motivating Learners

201 - Motivates by positive feedback, praise, and rewards
202 - Is responsive to the needs, aptitudes, talents, and learning styles of students
203 - Develops learning activities that are challenging to students
204 - Provides opportunities for student expression in music, drama, and other artistic forms
205 - Stimulates students to participate in class discussions and activities
206 - Generates a sense of enthusiasm among students
207 - Helps students experience social and intellectual satisfactions
208 - Relates achievement in school to life outside it
209 - Other (specify)

300 - Relationships with Students

301 - Collects pertinent information about students and maintains the confidentiality of it

FORM A, CONTINUED

300 - Relationships with Students, Continued

302 - Shows concern for students as individuals
303 - Counsels students individually and in groups
304 - Promotes an open atmosphere, enabling students to express their opinions
305 - Helps students develop positive self-concepts
306 - Encourages students to define realistic goals for themselves
307 - Is sensitive to the career needs of students
308 - Shows concern for students who have personal problems or handicaps
309 - Encourages students to strive for high achievement
310 - Enables students to make worthwhile contributions in class
311 - Utilizes the resources of pupil personnel-staff services
312 - Makes self available for conferences with students
313 - Guides students in the observance of democratic principles
314 - Promotes positive behavior patterns for students
315 - Manages behavior problems on an individual basis
316 - Has good rapport with students
317 - Treats causes, rather than symptoms, of situations that produce discord
318 - Is consistent and fair in dealing with students
319 - Shows warmth and understanding in dealing with students
320 - Shares concerns regarding students with colleagues and parents
321 - Other (specify)

400 - Utilizing Resources

401 - Is aware of available resources
402 - Uses a variety of available resources
403 - Uses physical school environment (both building and grounds) to support learning activities
404 - Adapts available resources to individual needs of students
405 - Uses the services of specialists available in the selection and utilization of resources
406 - Uses equipment and materials efficiently
407 - Other (specify)

500 - Instructional Techniques

501 - Encourages students to think
502 - Uses a variety of teaching techniques
503 - Uses a variety of instructional materials
504 - Varies opportunity for creative expression
505 - Helps students apply their experiences to life situations
506 - Conducts stimulating class discussions
507 - Encourages the development of individual interests and creative activities

FORM A, CONTINUED

500 - Instructional Techniques, Continued

508 - Uses appropriate evaluative techniques to measure student progress
509 - Assists students to evaluate their own growth and development
510 - Provides opportunities for students to develop leadership qualities
511 - Enables students to share in carrying out classroom activities
512 - Communicates with students individually and/or in groups
513 - Shows flexibility in carrying out teaching activities
514 - Creates an atmosphere of mutual respect between students and teacher
515 - Enables students to learn how to work independently and in groups
516 - Promotes group cohesiveness
517 - Uses feedback information skillfully
518 - Monitors the progress of students
519 - Other (specify)

600 - Professional Growth and Responsibility

601 - Participates in the development and implementation of school policies and procedures
602 - Maintains good rapport with colleagues
603 - Keeps self up to date in areas of specialization
604 - Takes advantage of in-service education opportunities
605 - Participates in school and systemwide committees
606 - Assists in out-of-class activities, including student management
607 - Shares ideas, materials, and methods with professional colleagues
608 - Shares in the evaluation of the effectiveness of educational programs
609 - Consults with previous teachers, team leaders, department heads, consultants, and specialists to improve the teaching-learning process
610 - Interprets school programs to parents and to the community as opportunities occur
611 - Other (specify)

700 - Relationships with Parents

701 - Gets parents to assist with school activities
702 - Encourages parents to visit the classes of the children
703 - Conducts constructive parent conferences
704 - Interprets learning programs to parents
705 - Stresses a positive approach in parent relations
706 - Maintains confidentiality in relations with parents
707 - Other (specify)

Identify Needs

Needs should be determined cooperatively by evaluatee and evaluator and should not be assumed to be only weaknesses. Needs also can be areas of strength in which further gains can be made. A useful way to identify needs is to regard them as areas to emphasize in order to attain the maximum degree of improvement in performance.

If this step is carried out informally and orally, in a one-to-one conference between evaluatee and evaluator, it will not be necessary to have a form for this purpose. If, on the other hand, it is desirable to conduct the identification of needs in a more structured manner and to have a written record of the process, a form for that purpose would be useful (see Form B).

Set Objectives and Action Plans

Traditional evaluation plans put considerable emphasis upon the assessment of personality, temperament, and character traits. Some plans call for a list of items and require the evaluator to indicate the evaluatee's status for each. For example, under the broad classification of staff relationships, there may be an item such as "Promotes friendly intraschool relationships." The evaluator is obliged to make estimates on a scale that indicates a high, average, or low rating. But how are accurate judgments to be made? Is it a matter of periodic classroom observation? Contact with the teacher outside the classroom? A general feeling about the matter? An educated guess? Perhaps all of these methods are assumed.

Another item on which teachers are sometimes judged is "Maintains sound emotional adjustment; is calm and mature in reactions." The individual and the evaluator often do not understand how this kind of assessment is made. The former may feel that reaching such a judgment involves an intrusion into personal areas. The evaluator may feel quite insecure in making an assessment that more validly could be in the domain of psychiatry than of school administration.

As a reaction against evaluating personality, temperament, and traits, some school systems have moved almost entirely in

FORM B

CHECK:
__Teacher
__Admin.

IDENTIFYING NEEDS

Evaluatee _____ Position_____

Evaluator _____ Position_____

School Year _____ Date _____

DIRECTIONS: Evaluatee lists number of descriptor(s) (Col. 2) that represents area(s) where improvement is needed. Evaluator lists number of descriptor(s) (Col. 3) that also indicate area(s) in which the Evaluatee should make improvement(s). In Col. 4 the two may indicate consensus. These will be needs that will be addressed during the evaluation period.

FOR TEACHERS				FOR ADMINISTRATORS			
Responsibility Criteria	Eval'tee	Eval'tor	CON-SENSUS	Responsibility Criteria	Eval'tee	Eval'tor	CON-SENSUS
Col. 1	Col.2	Col.3	Col.4	Col. 1	Col.2	Col.3	Col.4
100—Planning/ Organizing				100—Organ. & Admin.			
200—Motivating Learners				200—Communi-cations Manage.			
300—Relation-ships with Students				300—Personnel Manage.			
400— Utilizing Resources				400—Manage. of Students			
500—Instruc-tional Techniques				500—Manage. of In-struction			
600—Profes-sional Growth/ Develop.				600—Profession-al Growth/ Respons.			
700—Relation-ships with Parents				700—Manage. of Facilities			
OTHER (Specify)				800—Financial/ Business Manage.			
				900—Profession-al Comp./ Improv.			
				OTHER (Specify)			

Signatures:

_____   _____
       (Evaluatee)   (Evaluator)
Date of conference: _____   COPIES: Orig.: Eval'tee; Copy: Eval'tor

the opposite direction, evaluating achievement of performance objectives alone. With this approach, particular areas or problems of performance are identified. For example, a teacher may indicate a desire to improve discipline in the classroom. This is a real problem that has a direct bearing upon effectiveness in teaching. The teacher and the principal discuss the matter. They may agree that this calls for a single objective. An understanding is reached as to the procedure that will be followed to accomplish improvement. Agreement is reached about the way success or the lack of it is to be determined. At the end of the year, the evaluator, in cooperation with the teacher, will make a judgment about progress made in attaining desired results.

Evaluation, from this point of view, is conceived, planned, and carried out in a manner that puts a premium upon job performance. Objectives are established. Supervision and help are related to evaluation. Results are assessed at the end of the year. Personality traits may be factors in the final evaluation, but they are incidental rather than primary elements.

A precaution is necessary. One difficulty with the performance objectives concept of evaluation is that the focus may be on too narrow a range of specific activities and obvious areas of total performance that need attention may be ignored. This extreme is the exact opposite of the global nature of personality rating.

Obviously there is a middle ground. While there is much to be said for identifying specific objectives, it is important to understand that total performance must also be considered. This is why the nature of an individual's job must be clearly identified and defined. Evaluation should be based upon the specific areas of greatest need as well as upon all other aspects of the job.

After a particular problem is identified, an agreement is reached as to the procedure that will be used in working on the problem. The evaluation process involves: defining the problem, determining its scope and limitations, doing background reading on the subject, applying information gained from reading, checking on the results of these applications, sharing the results with others, keeping the evaluator informed as to progress that is being made, and making a final assessment.

It cannot be overemphasized that this kind of evaluation

takes time and effort. There are some who take the position that it requires too much of these precious qualities. There is reason to believe, however, that evaluation plans that are well designed and oriented toward the assessment of performance results will pay good dividends. Superficial evaluation based upon incidental contacts and cursory judgments may take less time, but it is doubtful that such evaluation can or does accomplish as much as evaluation based upon performance objectives.

It is important to decide whether to write performance objectives in general or behavioral terms. The former are less complicated, easier to write, and require less sophistication to implement. General objectives are more common, but they have disadvantages: they are not precise, implementing action is more difficult, and evaluation is more subjective. General objectives often cause a divergence of opinion between evaluatee and evaluator when evaluative estimates are made of the extent to which an objective has been achieved.

Objectives, behaviorally stated, should pinpoint concrete actions that will be required for their attainment. The responsibilities of the evaluatee and the evaluator can be more clearly defined. The emphasis is upon explicit action. Documentation of performance achievements and deficiencies tends to be easier when an objective is behaviorally stated. It does require greater skill to state performance objectives or targets in behavioral terms, as focusing too strongly upon the technical aspects of target formation may detract from the substance of the objective. Another disadvantage of designing behavioral objectives is that there is a special difficulty in formulating targets in the affective domain.

When establishing evaluation procedures, each school system should ponder the merits and demerits of both general goals and behavioral objectives in target formation. Time and circumstances will determine the best approach. It is important also to keep in mind that evaluation procedures can and should be reviewed periodically to determine modifications and refinements dictated by experience.

It is advisable to have a form on which the objective and the action plan to achieve it are stated so that both the evaluatee and the evaluator will understand what is to be done, the out-

FORM C (Separate Form C for   Teacher ___
         each objective)   OBJECTIVE/ACTION PLAN   Adm./Supv. ___

Evaluatee:_____ Position:_____

Evaluator:_____ Position:_____

School Year:_____ Date:_____

Number of Descriptor:_____

Objective: Be explicit. State desired outcome and method of measurement of results.

Action Plan: State steps or activities that will be conducted to achieve the objective. Also, indicate approximate date when each will be completed.

ASSESSMENT OF RESULTS: (To be completed by Evaluatee and reviewed by Evaluator)

Check - Objective was:

___ Fully Achieved
___ Partially Achieved (*)
___ Not Achieved (*)

Reviewed by Evaluator:

___ Concur with Evaluatee's Assessment
___ Don't concur (**)

(*) Explanations required; use separate sheet   (**) Explanations required; use separate sheet

Note: Attach Form Cs to Summative Evaluation Report (Form D). COPIES: Original to Evaluatee; Copy to Evaluator.

come desired, and the method of measurement that will be used to determine whether the objective has been attained (see Form C). By including space on the form for the evaluative results, it is easy to attach the form to the Summative Evaluation Report, thus avoiding the necessity of having to copy all the information on the latter form. A separate form should be used for each objective so there will be ample space to list implementing activities in the action plan. Using separate forms means that if there were four or five objectives, there would be that many copies of the form.

Carry Out Action Plan

The nature of the performance targets is influenced by the strategies that are devised to attain them. The plan of action is composed of those activities that the evaluatee and the evaluator have decided are the most promising for achieving the objective. The evaluatee and the evaluator have mutual interests in the successful achievement of the targets. The former has a direct and personal interest, and the latter has an interest that stems from management and supervisory responsibilities. Performance activities should be integrated into the supervisory program because these two processes are mutually reinforcing.

It is assumed that performance targets will have been carefully established and that each partner in the duet understands his role and responsibility for accomplishing the targets. The evaluatee, at the outset, obviously needs to know exactly what is expected. He needs to know how his job is being defined, the precise nature of the major job targets, and the procedures that are to be used to attain them. The evaluator should communicate to the evaluatee precisely what is expected of him.

When proper planning has taken place, it will be possible for the evaluatee to know precisely how to proceed in independent action during the year. The nature of the performance targets will determine which specific actions should be taken. The evaluator should determine the kinds of specific help to be given to and contacts to be made with the evaluatee during the year. It is very important that the evaluator interrelate supervisory and performance activities so that maximum results may be achieved.

The evaluatee also needs to clearly understand that evaluations and supervisory functions are mutually supportive during the year, and the evaluator has the responsibility of clarifying for the individual how he hopes to relate evaluation and supervision. This does not mean, of course, that all supervisory contacts have to be exclusively related to evaluation. There will be many contacts of an incidental as well as of a planned nature that will occur and grow out of the day-to-day instructional program. The point is that, wherever possible, evaluation and supervision should be related and should not be regarded as separate activities.

Monitoring Procedures

Once the details of the plan of action are understood and agreed upon, the process of implementation should get under way. Basic to the plan of action is the monitoring of the evaluatee's performance. The monitoring process is most helpful if very precise performance objectives have been formulated. These should be as relevant as possible for both short- and long-range needs of the individual. If there are clearly identified performance objectives, which have the capability of reasonable quantitative measurement, monitoring becomes much more relevant.

Monitoring procedures should be designed to comply with the following purposes and admonitions.

1. To collect relevant information. The object is to collect data rather than to evaluate it. The monitor is not necessarily the evaluator.
2. To obtain representative data, i.e., samplings of the full range of performance behavior.
3. To use a variety of techniques. No single procedure should be used exclusively.
4. To make sure that the individual being monitored understands what the monitor is trying to do—to monitor and not to evaluate.
5. To make sure the individual being monitored understands that he will be directly involved in the assessment of the

data, that the better and more comprehensive the monitoring procedures, the more likely it is that the data to be assessed will truly reflect the status of productivity.

It should be understood that monitoring techniques are designed primarily to collect relevant data without making assessments as to the quality of performance.

While much of the discussion about monitoring here is related to the evaluation cycle and final assessment, this emphasis in no way is intended to minimize the importance of monitored information to an immediate improvement of performance. There have been some interesting findings in other fields that indicate that an immediate feedback from monitoring can have a positive impact upon the quality of performance. In several instances, information obtained through monitoring revealed facts to be contrary to earlier speculation. The feedback was all that was needed to bring about a change in performance that greatly improved results. In other cases, the degree of success suggested by the monitored information stimulated confidence and encouragement, which led evaluatees to even higher performance levels.

General Practices Useful to Monitors

The number and type of monitoring techniques to be used should be decided upon by a committee on evaluation that represents the teaching staff as well as administrators and supervisors. Regardless of the techniques used, there are general practices that may be useful to the monitors.

Plan Carefully. It must be remembered that evaluation will not be effective unless adequate data, which are reasonably representative and relevant, have been secured. Careful planning is obviously of prime importance in collecting such data.

Establish Rapport. The key to the effectiveness of any one or all of the monitoring techniques is the degree of rapport that exists between the evaluatee and the evaluator. This should not be left to chance; it must be deliberately cultivated.

Schedule Monitoring Actions Carefully. If more than one technique is to be used, there should be good coordination and careful scheduling so that all the monitoring sessions will have purpose and relevance. While a general schedule may be established, it should be understood that deviations from it may be necessary, but these should be accomplished without undue frustration to the evaluatee.

Cycle of Monitoring Actions. It is difficult to prescribe a cycle to be used in conducting the monitoring techniques. It is important, however, that the data collected be as representative as possible of the total teaching performance and that it be as fair a representation as possible of the productivity of the individual.

Preparation for Each Activity. Regardless of the monitoring technique to be used, it is important that the people involved make adequate preparation so the purposes of monitoring are fulfilled.

Record Keeping. Most of the monitoring techniques should be designed to provide data that will not have to be interpreted or summarized by the monitor. In other words, forms and data sheets should be designed so that the monitor is able to record observations directly. It is important, however, to keep all of the data records so that a complete file will be available when it comes time to assess the data.

Open Communication. Perhaps the most important element in the monitoring process is open communication between the evaluatee and the monitor. There must be no hidden agenda. The evaluatee must understand that it is in his best interest that comprehensive and relevant data be collected so that the assessment of the data can be as valid as possible. As long as there is a clear understanding as to the objective of monitoring, it would seem that there should be no insurmountable barriers to the carrying out of this important component of the total evaluation process.

Assess Results

Evaluation is focused primarily upon the extent to which the performance objectives have been achieved. This does not preclude, however, the assessment of overall accomplishment. It is very important that there be a clear understanding between evaluatee and evaluator as to the bases upon which assessment will be made. If the objectives have been stated in behavioral terms, as has been suggested earlier, the nature of the assessments should be reasonably clear.

The mechanics of evaluation should be thoroughly discussed. The evaluation form should be clear and explicit. Evaluation records need to be adequate, but not overwhelming. Evaluators should make very clear how they plan to formulate their assessments. The timetable should be known by all involved. In short, the details related to the assessment stage must be clearly delineated.

Self-Evaluation

In true performance evaluation, self-assessment is an important part of the total process. If performance objectives have been established and if supervisory and evaluatee efforts have been expended in their fulfillment, then an assessment of accomplishments is necessary and should be a twofold process. The evaluatee needs to make a self-analysis and a judgment of results; likewise the supervisor must make an evaluation.

Self-evaluation, properly used, is a guide for planning further self-improvement. It is not a device for self-incrimination, providing damaging evidence that might be used by the supervisor to injure the evaluatee's professional status in some manner. Some teachers have, on occasion, viewed self-evaluation as self-indictment, but such an opinion suggests either a lack of understanding or a gross distortion of the process.

Assessment by Evaluator

This is a crucial aspect of the total process. The evaluator comes to that moment of truth when he must make a judgment as to the degree to which he believes the evaluatee has achieved success in attaining the established performance goals. Judgment must reflect a knowledge of what actually has transpired—including unforeseen circumstances that may have had an effect—a recognition of the amount of administrative and supervisory help given, and the nature of the results achieved.

Candor requires praise where due and criticism where warranted. Above all, evaluative estimates should be supported by evidence that observations were made, data were collected, conferences were held, and assistance was provided, all within a framework of fairness and objectivity.

Summative Evaluation Report

In addition to assessing the achievement of performance objectives, it is necessary to assess overall performance and to record the assessments on a Summative Evaluation Report (see Form D). Generally summative assessments are made by the evaluator. Consequently no specific provision is made on the suggested Summative Evaluation Report for self-assessments by the evaluatee, but should self-assessments be desired, they can be added.

It is important, if summative assessments are to be of maximum usefulness, for the evaluator to explain all less-than-satisfactory ratings. For this reason, a section should be provided for comments, and the same space may also be used for comments by the evaluatee. Generally the latter are optional, the decision being left to the evaluatee. In some instances, school systems wish to record indications of personnel actions called for as a result of the assessments. These recommendations for personnel action should also be indicated in the comments section of the Summative Evaluation Report.

Assessment Symbols

There are various ways to describe performance results, both for the achievement of objectives and for overall effectiveness in the major areas of responsibility. There are strengths and weaknesses in almost any type of symbols used. Some examples of assessment symbols, and their strengths and weaknesses, are given in Table 2.1 and Table 2.2.

Discuss Results

The reason many evaluation conferences are not too successful or rewarding, either for the evaluatee or for the evaluator, is that ample preparation is not made. Most evaluators agree that talking with an evaluatee about job performance is perhaps the most important part of the entire process. Yet it cannot be denied that frequently neither party looks forward to the evaluation conference.

FORM D

SUMMATIVE EVALUATION REPORT

CHECK:
__ Teacher
__ Admins.

Evaluatee _____ Position _____

Evaluator _____ Position _____

School Year _____

ASSESSMENT OF OVERALL PERFORMANCE (Only Evaluator assesses overall performance. ASSESSMENT KEY: EE = Exceptionally effective, with commendation; E = Effective; NS = Needs Strengthening; U = Unsatisfactory. (The latter two ratings require explanation in COMMENTS section.)

FOR TEACHERS:	ASSESSMENT
100 - Planning and Organizing	____
200 - Motivating Learners	____
300 - Relationships with Students	____
400 - Utilizing Resources	____
500 - Instructional Techniques	____
600 - Professional Growth and Responsibility..............	____
700 - Relationships with Parents	____

FOR ADMINISTRATORS:	ASSESSMENT
100 - Organization and Administration	____
200 - Communications Management	____
300 - Personnel Management	____
400 - Management of Students	____
500 - Management of Instruction	____
600 - Management of Services	____
700 - Management of Facilities	____
800 - Financial/Business Management	____
900 - Professional Competencies and Improvement	____

COMMENTS:
(If more space is needed, use reverse side)

SIGNATURES:

Evaluatee _____ Date _____

EVALUATOR _____ Date _____

(Signatures do not necessarily imply agreement, only that process was completed.) COPIES: Original - Central Office; Copy for Evaluatee and Copy for Evaluator.

Table 2.1

Assessment Symbols for Attainment of Objectives

Symbol Types	Strengths	Weaknesses
(1) A = Objective achieved NA = Objective not achieved	(a) Simple; up or down method of assessment (b) Encourages objectives that can be measured objectively	(a) Rigid (b) No provision for partial achievement
(2) A = Objective achieved PA = Objective partially achieved NA = Objective not achieved	(a) Clear-cut; easy to interpret (b) Encourages objectives that have measurability (c) Provides opportunity to show degrees of attainment	(a) Causes evaluator problems in deciding differences in two top rating symbols (b) Makes no provision for indicating that results were in excess of desired outcome(s)
(3) 5 = Results exceeded expected outcome(s) 4 = Results met expected outcome(s) 3 = Results partially met expected outcome(s) 2 = Results did not meet expected outcome(s) 1 = Results unsatisfactory	(a) Provides maximum flexibility in describing results (b) Numbers have explicit meanings (c) Compatible with conventional rating systems	(a) Too many ratings; not easy to make such distinctions in assessment (b) Likely to result in skewed ratings toward two top numbers
(4) Narrative Assessment: A concise statement of what actually took place during the year with an indication of the effectiveness of the results achieved	(a) Encourages more individualized assessments (b) Facilitates greater preciseness in stating that which actually occurred	(a) Contributes to the writing of ambiguous assessments (b) Time-consuming

Table 2.2

Assessment Symbols for Overall Performance

Symbol Types	Strengths	Weaknesses
(1) E = Overall performance effective I = Overall performance ineffective	(a) Requires evaluator to make definite estimates of effectiveness	(a) Rigid; difficult to show degrees of effectiveness (b) Strong temptation to give a preponderance of E ratings (c) Frequently not well received by either evaluatee or evaluator
(2) E = Overall performance effective NS = Performance needs strengthening U = Performance unsatisfactory	(a) Conventional; realistic (b) Easy to pinpoint areas needing improvement	(a) Not possible to show exemplary performance (b) No way to show a degree of effectiveness between two top ratings
(3) 5 = Exemplary (unusually effective) performance 4 = Excellent performance 3 = Satisfactory performance 2 = Below satisfactory performance 1 = Unsatisfactory performance	(a) More latitude for estimating effectiveness (b) Very conventional; easily understood	(a) Too many shades of difference (b) Likely there will be an excessive number of 4 and 5 ratings (c) Makes rater bias more of a possibility
(4) Narrative Statement: The evaluator writes a summary statement that will give an overall assessment of the effectiveness of the evaluatee in the major areas of responsibility	(a) Encourages more individualized assessments (b) Facilitates greater preciseness in stating that which actually occurred	(a) Contributes to the writing of ambiguous assessments (b) Time-consuming

Preparation for the conference need not be difficult or time-consuming, provided the evaluator has done a good job throughout the year of collecting as much performance data as possible, making certain that adequate help was provided, and keeping adequate records of contacts. While good preplanning should be stressed, it should be well understood that conferences do not always go as planned. There are no set rules for success. Flexibility and perception are required of the evaluator.

The emphasis of evaluation conferences should not be solely on discussing problems. On the contrary, the conference more properly is a place where progress is discussed and understanding is sought. Conference discussions usually include

> Discussion of long- and short-range goals and objectives
> Recognition of good work
> Mutual exchange of suggestions for improvement
> Selection of top-priority job tasks or job targets
> Clarification of the responsibilities of both parties
> Correction of misinformation and misunderstanding
> A myriad of other topics that may seem important to either party at that particular time

Again, the best recipe for conducting a good conference is ample preparation. There is a measure of security in knowing that all the evaluator's obligations during the evaluation period have been fulfilled. This definitely will contribute to the success of the conference. The biggest contributor, however, is experience. Only after many conferences have been conducted with all kinds of evaluatees are evaluators likely to feel reasonably confident and sure of themselves in the conference.

Follow-up

The conference is likely to yield some ideas for action, and follow-up will be required. If it appears that the evaluator should give some follow-up help or assistance, make sure that commitments are made realistically. Do not make promises that cannot be kept.

It is usually a good idea for the evaluator, following the conference, to make some notes about what was agreed upon, what commitments were made by both evaluator and evaluatee, and other
ideas for follow-through. The record is important. It is easy to
forget what was said in a conference as the rush of later events
and pressures of other duties often dim recollections of what
transpired. Simple notes, easily accessible in the evaluatee's folder,
become valuable for making sure follow-up action is completed.

Observations Concerning the Evaluation Process

When improved performance is the object of evaluation, it
is clear that an overemphasis upon criticism deters improvement.
It certainly retards the accomplishment of performance targets.
Experience shows also that improved performance is stimulated
when specific objectives, rather than general goals, are the focus
of effort.

More frequent contacts between evaluatee and evaluator tend
to increase the effectiveness of the evaluation process. The type
of evaluation that puts a premium upon goal setting, a continued
working together, and an assessment of results produced is likely
to yield a more favorable attitude on the part of the evaluatee
and facilitate achievement of the overall purpose of evaluation—
the improvement of performance.

Human problems and concerns are constantly present in the
school setting. Teachers may be problems to administrators;
administrators can be problems to teachers. Fortunately there
are solutions that usually work reasonably well provided there is
mutual goodwill and a common effort between teachers and
principals. Generally solutions can be found that do not entail
performing "basic surgery" upon the personality of either the
teacher or the principal. The performance-oriented type of
evaluation has built-in communication features that help to
minimize abrasive situations.

Good evaluation procedures, well-designed forms, and
explicit directions are essential, but unless they are applied
skillfully the ultimate results may fall well below reasonable
expectations. In order for an evaluator to increase his skills

in evaluating either teachers or administrative personnel, he needs a clear understanding of the purposes, possibilities, and procedures of the evaluation process. Efforts need to be made to show evaluators—and evaluatees—that, first, evaluation is a process to clarify duties and responsibilities, improve performance, promote professional growth, facilitate better communication, and foster job satisfaction. Second, they should also understand that evaluation can

1. Improve the quality of educational services for students; clarify the expectations of evaluators
2. Encourage the establishment of more pertinent job targets or objectives
3. Bring about a closer working relationship between the person being evaluated and the person doing the evaluating
4. Enable the evaluatee to understand better how those who provide direction and supervision feel about his work

Third, the evaluation process, in simple terms, involves

1. Setting job targets—clarifying needs, setting priorities, and understanding better how targets relate to total job performance
2. Making supervision and evaluation more compatible—seeing the relationship between the two functions and understanding how each can complement the other
3. Making self-assessments—examining the purposes and usefulness of self-evaluation as an important part of the total process
4. Improving assessments by evaluators—analyzing the techniques of making a valid evaluation based upon "evidence" rather than upon "speculation"
5. Conducting evaluation conferences—considering what goes into an effective conference and understanding that a poor one can do a great deal of harm
6. Planning appropriate follow-up action—outlining actions that should be taken to promote the development of the individual; good follow-up actions constitute the out-

comes of evaluation and are the dividends for the time and effort put into the process

It has been said that *what* is done in evaluation is important, but *how* it is accomplished is crucial. Outcomes are more likely to be positive if the six actions indicated above are carried out with care and sensitivity.

3

Evaluation of Teachers

Orientation and training provided by the principal are essential steps to good teacher evaluation. Beginning with the first meeting of the principal and a new teacher, the orientation should cover the school plant, school personnel, and school policies, the abilities of the pupils, the nature of the school community, and the activities of the parent groups. All of this information will be helpful to the teacher in thinking and planning.

As soon as the class work begins, problems are sure to arise, especially for new and beginning teachers. In solving these, with the aid of the principal, much can and should be done to determine the teacher's needs and capabilities to successfully do the work.

When the evaluation plan is introduced, a careful explanation of the development of the entire process should be made. Some teachers may have a tendency to view evaluation as a rating process. This should be anticipated and careful steps should be taken to explain fully the meaning and implications of performance evaluation—the significance of developing performance objectives and the results to be achieved. The meaning of self-analysis and its relationship to the evaluation by the administrator also needs careful explanation. The principal should strive to reduce possible fear, apprehension, and confusion in the mind of the teacher. In other words, the establishment of a climate of acceptance is paramount.

Classroom visits by the principal and the immediate supervisor and the counsel they can then offer will do much to help teachers see themselves as they work at the job.

Thus, when the time comes for the conference, the teachers will have a base for an understanding of their performance.

Responsibility Criteria

As indicated in Chapter 2, it is useful to develop a list of duties and responsibilities to serve as the starting point in the evaluation cycle. Teachers and evaluators should have a clear understanding of what is expected for each broad area of responsibility, described as on Form A, and the importance of each.

Area 100—Planning and Organizing

Teachers have many planning and organizing responsibilities. Logistical skill is required to organize youngsters into appropriate learning groups, and materials and supplies must be organized, deployed, and used wisely. The organizational structure may present constraints or facilitate performance. New techniques such as the open classroom, ungradedness, differentiated staff structure, and flexible scheduling procedures put a premium upon the managerial skill of the teacher. The use of teacher aides and volunteers involves planning, organization, and delegation of work.

As evaluatees, teachers are obliged to diagnose their competencies in planning and organizing. They may wish to improve one or more aspects of their performance in these areas; if so, they can develop performance objectives to help attain these ends.

Area 200—Motivating Learners

The use of feedback, praise, and reward are essential elements of motivation. Responsiveness to learning needs, aptitudes, and learning styles of students cannot be overemphasized. The ability to generate an enthusiasm for learning is also part of the motivation process.

Area 300—Relationships with Students

Successful teachers are much more than purveyors of subject matter. In counseling students, they are obliged to know their students' backgrounds and needs, and it is not possible to esti-

mate the worth of a friendly and concerned teacher's willingness to take the time to counsel a youngster about educational
and related problems. Sometimes the constructive and supportive
influence of an adult friend has more to do with the effective
education of a pupil than any other aspect of the total learning
experience.

The value of counseling puts a high premium on those teachers
who are inclined to give ample time to individual pupils who
need help. For some students, the counseling may consist of
encouraging them to engage in individualized instruction projects,
to go ahead on their own, to explore for themselves, to become
resourceful, independent learners. For others, it may be patient,
sustained help in the solving of personal or home problems that
affect the learning process.

Consultation with pupils affords that personal touch in teaching that humanizes education by making learning an individualized as well as a group process. It is a quality that is highly
prized by those people who are most supportive of education.

Area 400—Utilizing Resources

An awareness of and an effective use of the resources—human
and material—available for instructional purposes are necessary
attributes of good teaching. Being able to adapt available resources to individual needs is a part of effective teaching.

Area 500—Instructional Techniques

The instructional responsibilities of teachers are of prime
significance when considering the total job. The specific nature
of the activities that compose instruction must be identified.
Performance effectiveness may be judged with reference to the

> Extent and quality of basic preparation
> Degree to which knowledge is current and abreast of trends
> Evidence of effective planning
> Ability to organize instructional and administrative pro-
> cedures
> Recognition of differences in the capacities and interests
> of pupils
> Extent to which techniques are resourceful and innova-
> tive

Some students may be oriented toward college, and every effort has to be made to get them ready and able to be admitted to the college of their choice. Instruction for those students must be highly challenging and will require, on the part of the teacher, a continuing effort to keep abreast of new knowledge and instructional procedures, which are increasing rapidly. Other students may not be college bound, and preparation for some type of technical/vocational post-high-school training becomes of paramount concern for those students. Such preparation requires no less of a need for strong instructional skill and competency although the emphases may be different.

Each teacher, with assistance from the evaluator, has to think about the varying instructional requirements of his particular assignments and identify those aspects or activities of instruction that are inherent in it. The teacher and the evaluator can then identify those aspects that need strengthening and can design performance objectives that, they hope, will yield the outcomes desired.

Area 600—Professional Growth and Responsibility

Professional development is a major area for improvement through evaluation. Increasing technical skills, gaining more conceptual knowledge in an area of specialization, increasing human relations competence, keeping up to date, learning new techniques, preparing for advancement and promotion, and other similar pursuits provide the subject matter of in-service growth. Evaluation can be an important means of stimulating professional development.

In-service training in education frequently is regarded as a kind of beneficial salve to be applied without particular regard to the quality, efficiency, or appropriateness of the instruction. Credit rather than content often is considered most important. An analytical approach to the major areas of teaching and administration through performance evaluation may well be a sound means of eliminating the abuses of conventional in-service education practices. In-service development according to individual needs, as suggested by performance evaluation, strikes at the superficiality of present practices.

Another significant area for teachers is that of professional participation, which means being willing to contribute time and knowledge to the development of curricular materials and organization so that the educational program may be enhanced. Participation can mean a willingness to develop better individual classroom teaching materials or service in groups and on committees that are developing instructional materials for the system as a whole.

Professional participation embraces many activities connected with problem solving. Difficult educational problems need attention and study today, and teachers have much to contribute to the solution of these perplexing problems. They are well advised to participate on many kinds of committees and in groups that are studying educational problems and seeking better solutions to them.

Area 700—Relationships with Parents

The parents' interest in their children's educational adjustment and progress varies greatly and depends upon many factors. Those parents who prize education highly tend to want continuing contacts with their youngsters' teachers and principals. Liaison with the home, in such instances, is usually closer and more supportive than in those situations where the parents' interest is low or nonexistent and may reflect more the initiative of the parents than of the teacher or the principal.

Previous experiences that parents have had with schools may have been negative. Such conditions influence teacher-parent contacts and can make them difficult. On the other hand, skillful communication and interaction can yield great rewards even in difficult situations.

Obviously the teacher and the evaluator must assess the climate of school-parent relations and carefully plan contacts with parents, and this can be a substantial variable in the teaching job.

Identify Needs

The way needs are identified will vary depending upon the preferences of evaluatees and evaluators and the procedures that may have been developed by different school systems. As a possible approach, identifying needs may follow the sequences indicated below.

EVALUATEE	EVALUATOR
1. Reviews the performance criteria and/or job description (where applicable)	1. Reviews the performance criteria and/or job description (where applicable)
2. Seeks suggestions from supervisors (and optionally from students or parents)	2. Considers observed needs of evaluatee (based upon past performance)
3. Makes tentative determinations of those needs for which objectives and action plans may be written	3. Makes tentative determinations of those needs that can be discussed with evaluatee
4. Contacts evaluator to arrange a time and place to discuss needs, possible objectives, and action plans	4. Participates with evaluatee in a planning conference to agree on needs, objectives, and action plans

Set Objectives and Action Plans

It would be foolish to assume that the personality factors have no bearing upon successful performance in teaching. Personality traits, habits, and the manner in which a teacher gets along with pupils, parents, and colleagues have an important bearing upon performance outcomes. Judgment, emotional stability, initiative, tact, and courtesy are certainly important in teaching; the difficulty is they are hard to evaluate. The evaluator, in most instances, must make very subjective judgments, and an insecure person finds it difficult to accept criticism and often becomes defensive when the evaluation on these points is negative. Much skill also is required on the part of an evaluator to explain the reasons for a negative assessment.

Experience indicates that such evaluation is more effective when the emphasis is upon performance. If personality traits have a bearing upon job effectiveness, they can be dealt with not as separate entities but as a part of the total performance. This approach calls for some definitions and agreements at the outset. Success criteria are necessary, and these should be developed in specific terms and focused upon desired results.

It is possible for an individual and his evaluator to pinpoint performance objectives or targets that may be used as the basis for evaluation at the culmination of the year's work. It has been noted that instructional procedures may be an area of major emphasis, and individual teachers can identify a number of specific problems related to their classroom instruction. These problems, then, should get primary attention during the year. It should be understood, however, that the final assessment is not necessarily limited to the specific problems identified at the beginning of the year. The whole gamut of the individual's work will be reviewed.

It must be admitted that there still is some degree of subjectivity in the evaluation of job performance as well as in the assessment of the personal qualities of an individual. Subjective judgment is not necessarily bad, but it does require a good understanding between the individual and the evaluator about the ground rules the latter will use in making the judgment. Evaluation is more effective, however, if reliance upon purely subjective judgment can be kept to a minimum and if greatest dependence can be placed upon performance data. This applies not only to evaluating achievement of specific job targets but also to evaluating all aspects of total performance.

Performance objectives may be stated in terms of behavioral change or productivity gains. The former are commonly believed to be more feasible than the latter. If behavioral change is to be the objective, the question is whether change in the teacher's behavior or that of pupils will be sought. Perhaps both. What types of change? Adaptations in teaching style and techniques? Better planning? Greater flexibility and adjustability? Increased emphasis upon innovation and creativity? More realistic assessment of student achievement? The list can be extended to include a wide variety of behavioral change, but behavioral change in the cognitive domain is much more common than in affective areas. It is quite possible that some performance objectives might be centered in the area of change in pupil behavior. If so, performance targets might include improved attitudes toward school, a better attendance record, more effective study habits, or development of a particular interest in some aspect of the school's program.

If performance goals include productivity gains as well as

behavioral change, it is possible to concentrate upon both evaluatee and pupil accomplishment. Examples of the former might be additional training or acquisition of new skills in a particular area, improved techniques in managerial and organizational skills, implementation of new teaching procedures, or successfully carrying out a research project related to some aspect of the assignment. Pupil productivity gains are likely to be expressed in terms of increased achievement. Traditionally, teachers have not been receptive to basing evaluations of their performance upon measures of pupil achievement, especially when these are confined to achievement-test scores. This area deserves reexamination, however, and the increasing demand for accountability makes this reexamination necessary.

Once performance goals have been established, each objective, and the action plan devised to achieve it, should be written down on a form provided for that purpose (see Figure 3.1). These written statements can then be referred to when evaluation takes place.

Monitoring Procedures and Techniques

Very frequently traditional monitoring consists basically of inspection visits by the evaluator to observe the teacher at work in the classroom. It is argued that the greater the number of visits and the degree to which they show the teacher to the best advantage, the more likely evaluation assessments will be accurate and reflect the true state of instructional excellence.

A typical sequence in evaluator-teacher interaction is observation, evaluation, and conference. This process presumes that

1. The teacher is the primary agent—plans and carries out the instructional process.
2. The evaluator is the secondary agent—observes, assesses, and confers relative to effectiveness of instruction.
3. Observations yield the kind of information required to make valid evaluations.
4. The evaluator is expert enough to make a confident assessment of the effectiveness of instruction.
5. The teacher accepts the evaluator's expertise.
6. Evaluator-teacher rapport is unquestioned.

Figure 3.1

Example of Objective and Action Plan

Teacher ___
Adm./Supv. ___

Evaluatee:_____ Position:_____

Evaluator:_____ Position:_____

School Year:_____ Date:_____

Number of Descriptor:_____502_____

Objective: Be explicit. State desired outcome and method of measurement of results.

I will increase my effectiveness in using instructional materials, supplies, and techniques so that at the end of an introductory unit in science, 85 percent of my students will achieve instructional objectives in metric measurement and the forming of tenable hypotheses regarding class demonstrations. Results will be measured by a practical laboratory test prepared by the teacher.

Action Plan: State steps or activities that will be conducted to achieve the objective. Also, indicate approximate date when each will be completed.

1. Students will witness a series of demonstrations and describe what they see, learning to distinguish between collecting data and writing a conclusion. (To be completed during first week)

2. Students will be blindfolded for some of the above demonstrations.

3. A science-math team-teaching approach to the decimal system and the metric system of measurement will help students learn how to use a metric ruler.

4. Students will use household items to judge length, weight, and volume in the metric system. (All during the time the introductory unit is being taught)

5. After seeing the teacher set up an activity, "hands on" experiment, students will predict plausible hypotheses and perform tests to check if theirs is the correct one. (By the end of the period)

ASSESSMENT OF RESULTS: (To be completed by Evaluatee and reviewed by Evaluator)

Check - Objective was:

___ Fully Achieved
___ Partially Achieved (*)
___ Not Achieved (*)

Reviewed by Evaluator:

___ Concur with Evaluatee's Assessment
___ Don't Concur (**)

(*) Explanations required; use separate sheet (**) Explanations required; use separate sheet

Note: Attach Form Cs to Summative Evaluation Report (Form D). COPIES: Original to Evaluatee; Copy to Evaluator.

It is not argued here that these conditions cannot or may not exist in school systems. They frequently do, especially if the evaluator has attained expertise in the field and is accepted by the teacher as one who is especially capable of making assessments.

With the great proliferation of knowledge in teaching today, however, it is difficult for even the most expert evaluator to claim expertise in all phases of instruction. It is also likely that some teachers will be doubtful that their evaluators are sufficiently expert in assessment techniques to make valid evaluations. When evaluators face these conditions as they pursue their responsibilities as monitors and assessors, the question becomes one of how to achieve more effective monitoring.

Administrative Observations

In many school systems the only person available to observe the performance of teachers is the principal. This poses some very real problems, particularly at the secondary level, because in many instances the principal may not have sufficient knowledge of the subject being taught to be an effective observer. If performance objectives have been established in areas other than the teacher's specialty, however, the principal may be a very effective monitor. Furthermore, as a generalist, the principal has expertise in the techniques of instruction, planning and organization, management, and overall presentation of material. If the principal and the teacher have agreed upon the kinds of observations that would be most helpful, and if the principal concentrates on his own area of competence as a general leader, there is no doubt that he can be very effective as a monitor of teaching behavior.

When the monitor is an instructional supervisor or the head of a department in the area of the teacher's specialization, observations take on quite a different complexion. An instructional specialist, especially, is able to be more of a diagnostic observer, not only in collecting relevant data but also in formulating ideas that can be used later to assist the teacher in the improvement of his performance.

Self-Monitoring

Although not completely accepted by all authorities as a

viable process of evaluation, self-assessment does have consider-able merit. Those who say self-evaluation is of limited value point to the difficulty of an evaluatee to be completely candid, the tendency for highly competent evaluatees to underestimate themselves, and an equally noticeable tendency for less com-petent evaluatees to overevaluate themselves.

The process does have positive qualities, however. It can be used as a guide for self-improvement; it may be used as a tool for self-analysis and may be employed also as an instrument to identify the steps that may be taken to accomplish improve-ment. Certainly an individual's own perceptions as to what is happening, what is working out well, and what is not achieving the desired results are important bits of data that need to be taken into consideration when assessment time comes.

Trained Observers

There is a possibility that trained observers who are neither principals nor supervisors may be used as monitors. For example, student teachers and other students who are in teacher training might be taught how to observe teaching behavior and record significant data that would be useful to the evaluatee and the evaluator in making assessments of productivity.

Monitoring by trained observers could be initiated by the teacher as well as by an administrator or a supervisor. In general, the observations would be focused upon particular aspects of teaching behavior, and evaluatees and evaluators could coopera-tively develop forms or checklists that could be used by the trained observers to collect data. So long as the evaluatee and the evaluator are in full agreement as to the purpose of using trained observers in the classroom, this technique seems to offer some promise for adding to the data collected for the purpose of making an estimate of the degree of productivity.

Electronic Monitoring

Teachers, traditionally, have viewed electronic monitoring equipment as being a threat rather than an aid to instruction. But times are changing, and some teachers now use tape recorders as a monitoring technique. The teacher controls the use of the tape recorder, turning it on at significantly important times and using it to record teaching behavior. The tape recorder provides

examples of teaching practices for diagnosis. Although it repro-
duces only sound, a tape recorder is handy to use and easily
available.

Many school systems have purchased videotaping equipment,
and occasionally this is used as a monitoring technique. It has
the distinct advantage of being able to reproduce both sight and
sound, but its use becomes a production in that an operator
must be in the room. If proper orientation and explanations
are given, however, students become accustomed to the equipment. Videotaping permits the collection of important samplings
of practice and an accumulation of longitudinal sequences of
teaching behavior, making it possible to observe the progression
of teaching practices over a considerable period of time.

Assess Results

Self-Evaluation

Requiring teachers to assess themselves, as has been stated, is
not universally accepted by authorities. There are those who
hold that the process is an ineffective procedure. They say
teachers are likely to give an inaccurate estimate of themselves
because of an inability to be completely candid about their
strengths, weaknesses, achievements, or lack of accomplishment. Those who oppose self-evaluation maintain also that competent teachers, emotionally mature and secure, tend to under-
evaluate themselves and that those who are marginal or weak
in performance, or insecure, are prone to overestimate their
accomplishments. Opponents say self-evaluation is a relatively unreliable measure of competence and, therefore, its
usefulness as a tool in the evaluative process is open to serious
question.

Those people who are in favor of self-evaluation respond by
saying that self-evaluation can be a very effective instrument of
evaluation and that the inadequacies enumerated above result
from misuse of the self-assessment process and not necessarily
from any basic weakness in the technique itself. The apparent
inability of some teachers to assess their own performance may
stem from a misunderstanding of the real purpose of self-
evaluation. It may also result from the impression that the pro-

cess is used for old-fashioned rating purposes rather than as a means of promoting better performance.

Assessment by Evaluator

Whether or not the evaluator should use a teacher's self-assessment when formulating his own evaluation of that teacher is debatable. One possible advantage of seeing the teacher's estimate of his own performance is that it gives the evaluator a point of reference and enables him to modify his own judgments somewhat so they are in accordance with those of the teacher. (This may not necessarily be an advantage, however.) But making a completely independent evaluation, entirely divorced from the teacher's self-assessment, appears to have many advantages. It is probably a more valid judgment, evaluators are required to rely on their own best judgment supported by "facts," it is fairer to the evaluatee, it requires greater candor, and it is more likely to accomplish the goal of the evaluative process, the improvement of performance.

Preparation for making the evaluation consists of a thoughtful analysis of the job targets selected, a careful record of contacts made, anecdotal notes and other data related to observational visits, notes about help provided and conferences held, and a meaningful interpretation of all data.

Discussing Results

Many experienced teachers have been helpful over the years in pointing out some dimensions of a good principal-teacher relationship that are indispensable for a profitable and rewarding evaluation conference. The guidelines that follow are not all-inclusive, but they may be useful to evaluators as they prepare to hold evaluation conferences with their teachers.

1. Avoid the "boss complex."
2. Clarify the roles of evaluator and evaluatee in the evaluation setting.
3. Seek to establish that both parties should be primarily concerned with the educational welfare of the pupils rather than their own self-interest.

4. Be conscious that the evaluator's personality, as well as that of the evaluatee, will have an influence—good or bad—upon achievable results in the conference.
5. Strive for unity in leadership effort and action among all administrators in the building.
6. Be willing to let teachers express their feelings in the conference without risk of censure or reprisal even if they may be markedly different from those of the evaluator.
7. Provide for privacy.
8. Safeguard the confidential nature of any matter requiring it.
9. Avoid asking for opinions on the spot; allow the evaluatee time for consideration.
10. Strive for a climate of mutual respect.
11. Be prepared to take as well as to give.
12. Be honestly committed to the concept that teacher, principal, and supervisor are members of a team working for a good educational program.
13. Take the initiative in encouraging the teacher to make constructive criticisms.
14. Provide an opportunity for the discussion of school problems.
15. Invite suggestions; when made, try to do something about them.
16. Don't give a teacher the brush-off when problems are presented.
17. Try to be aware of what teachers are doing in their classes; be conversant with general developments in their fields of specialization but leave the discussion of technical aspects to the supervisor.
18. Don't talk too much; don't let the teacher talk too little.

Follow-up and Postconference Activities

During the conference, the teacher may see the need for certain kinds of follow-up activities to reinforce actions taken during the year. Pinpoint these and decide what should be done about them.

In the postconference activities, the supervisor and the

principal have a joint responsibility to the teacher being evaluated. This means that the principal should help the supervisor understand what has transpired as a result of the evaluation conference and that the supervisor should share with the administrator his reactions and observations. Areas to be worked on or an outline of the goals set may be written down with copies made for the three persons involved.

Every effort should be made to make the teacher feel that success is desired by all concerned and is possible through combined effort. From time to time evidence of improvement should be discussed to offer further encouragement. If success is not forthcoming, reassignment may be necessary. This reassignment may include a change of schools, subject area, age level, and/or ability level. However, all avenues of in-service training should be explored before other steps are taken.

The type or types of postconference activities planned for a teacher should correlate with the specific problems revealed through the evaluation conference. As the principal has daily contact with the evaluatee, he may learn of the latter's particular interests or talents and call the supervisor's attention to them. The efficient teacher should be given an opportunity to serve on systemwide committees or in activities that will utilize his talents. On the other hand, a weak teacher may gain understanding and strength through serving on such a committee. The organization of local school study groups or a series of meetings to study a school problem—such as noontime activities or the use of sets of supplementary books—may give the satisfactory teacher an opportunity to assume a leadership role. When the principal or supervisor shows an interest and takes an active part in such meetings, the teacher catches this spark. The administrator gains insight and understanding and shares common knowledge with the teacher which is useful for a discussion of the problems.

In-Service Opportunities

A teacher's improvement in teaching methods and techniques or better understanding of ways of working with children may come as a result of participation in some of the following in-service opportunities.

School District In-Service Program. The analysis of performance evaluation follow-up actions should provide a sound
basis for the in-service program of the district, and most individual school in-service programs could profit also. For instance,
customized training aids can be developed for those teachers
with common needs.

Individual or Small Study Groups Within the School. Conferences with principals, assistant principals, counselors, visiting
teachers, or supervisors can result in valuable information or
suggestions for teachers working on a specific problem. Sometimes small groups of teachers studying together gain the insight and perspective necessary for the solution of a given
problem.

Visiting Other Classes. This activity may take the form of
planned visiting days on which a teacher visits a colleague in
another school who is conducting a similar class and whose
approach offers positive suggestions for improvement in the
area needing attention. This technique is especially valuable for
the teacher whose ability to profit from oral or written suggestions is limited. Visitation may also be informal in situations
where a teacher has an opportunity to visit a strong teacher in
his own building. Preplanning with that teacher helps produce
better results from the visitation. Also, a follow-up conference
between the visiting teacher and his principal or supervisor
should be held to evaluate the help received. An effort should
be made to lessen the feeling on the part of some that a visiting
day is arranged only for teachers who have improvement needs.

Committee Work. This type of activity may be confined to
the study of instructional problems within the school, or it may
be systemwide in nature. Participation in the selection of text-
books or supplementary books, in the review of audiovisual aids
or other equipment or materials, or in the development of
curriculum guides encourages teachers to try new teaching aids
and methods and helps broaden their understanding of the educational process. Work on systemwide committees also brings
teachers into closer contact with other capable teachers and
offers opportunities for the development of leadership.

University Courses. Formal university courses can sometimes
offer excellent help, especially for the teacher who has returned

to teaching after a period of time away from the profession and also for the teacher who needs to update his knowledge of the subject matter and teaching techniques.

Informal or Individual Study. Suggested-reading lists in current professional periodicals or in reference books for teachers, bulletins, or newsclippings aid the teacher in directing individual study toward worthwhile purposes. Reference books for teachers, selected from the supplementary-books list, should be available in the principal's office, in the school library, or through the district or public library.

Close Association with a Capable Teacher. Assigning a beginning or an inefficient teacher to an experienced and skillful staff member may be, in some cases, more instrumental in bringing about improvement than any other technique. This plan is especially helpful for teachers who profit most from direct example.

Workshops. Well-planned workshops can help participants concentrate their attention on a particular problem and offer a method of acquiring understanding and useful information in a relatively short period of time. These meetings also help those who attend increase their abilities to contribute as a leader or as a member of a group.

Professional Organizations. Belonging to professional organizations and participating in local, state, or national meetings give teachers the feeling of being a part of something bigger than their own classrooms. The interest and pride in professional activities generated by these activities are reflected in the improved quality of teaching in the classroom.

Summary of Postevaluation Action

In summary, good postevaluation action involves

> Agreeing upon specific follow-up activities,
> Clarifying the responsibilities of both the teacher and the evaluator for carrying out commitments for action,
> Keeping informal notes and records of expressed proposals and subsequent implementing actions,
> Encouraging the teacher who has completed a periodic evaluation to continue self-action during the interim

until the next formal assessment for performance
improvement,

Keeping in touch with the teacher who is making an effort
to improve in order to show an interest in his efforts
and a personal concern for his achievements,

Being prepared to provide counsel and help as called for,

Encouraging all teachers to seek counsel from the evaluator any time they feel the need of it.

Teacher-Evaluator Relationship

A good working relationship between teacher and evaluator
is indispensable to an effective educational program. Does
evaluation of teaching performance enhance or hinder that
working relationship? It probably does both, depending upon
the nature of the procedure. A good working relationship is
likely to be hindered when the following conditions prevail:
(1) the purposes and processes of evaluation are confused or
obscure, (2) the teacher feels uncertain and insecure about his
role in the evaluation process and, more specifically, that the
process is being used in some harmful way, (3) the evaluator
conceives of evaluation as an inspectional and rating process,
and (4) communication between the teacher and the evaluator
is inadequate or practically nonexistent.

Evaluation tends to strengthen and enhance the teacher-
evaluator relationship when: (1) the opposite of the four previously mentioned conditions prevails, (2) improved performance
is the chief objective of the process, (3) teacher and evaluator
put the emphasis upon performance—what the teacher does or
what he is supposed to do—rather than upon personal qualities
and behavior, and (4) evaluation is as much as possible a cooperative process—the teacher has a definite role to perform and so
does the evaluator.

Particularly in the job target type of performance evaluation,
the face-to-face conferences between teacher and evaluator are
of crucial importance. Failure at this point negates much of the
value of the entire procedure. It is essential that there be a
radarlike awareness of the problems and concerns of teachers.
Both new and experienced teachers have problems and concerns,

and sometimes they cannot solve their problems without assistance. A sensitivity to those problems, especially before an acute stage has been reached, is one of the principal's more important obligations. This does not mean an unhealthy paternalism; it is the mark of a good executive. He must have an awareness that people have many concerns about their work as well as themselves, and the principal must also be able and willing to help with them. Properly used, evaluation based on achievement of performance objectives can help with the identification of problems and with their solutions.

4

Evaluating Administrators
and Supervisors

Most discussions about evaluation deal with teachers simply because teachers make up the vast bulk of the professional work force of a school district. They also have the greatest and most direct "client contact" with students and many parents. But when teacher evaluation is discussed, almost invariably the question of evaluation of administrators is also raised. Who is going to evaluate the evaluators? This question is often asked by teachers who only want to make certain that administrators, too, share in the discomfort, potential unfairness, and superficiality of traditional rating programs. However, many people are sincerely interested in precisely how administrative and supervisory positions, general and specialized, may be evaluated. It is obvious that the nature of these positions is quite different from that of the classroom instructor.

One of the major advances possible when an evaluation program based on performance objectives is used is that the same basic principles and procedures can be applied whether the professional assignment is in the classroom, in administration, or in some specialized assignment. Responsibility criteria and the objectives approach afford the flexibility and "customizing" qualities necessary to validly assess the performance of those in positions that may differ greatly in specifics but are all part of one complex process.

Evaluating Specialists

The evaluation program for those people who are in specialized positions may require some modifications and adjustments depending upon the nature of the particular job. The services performed may be of such a highly specialized nature or be so diverse that use of the rating type of evaluation procedures may seem improbable. There is likely to be considerably more challenge in setting up criteria to assess the quality of performance on the basis of objectives. This is not to say that difficulty should be equated with impossibility. In the setting of objectives, for example, it may be necessary for the evaluator to become much more intimately acquainted with the specialized aspects of the position being evaluated.

When services are performed over a broad geographic area and for equally widely distributed recipients, it may be necessary to make special provisions for data monitoring and in the evaluation procedure itself. For example, a primary evaluator may have assistance from persons who are recipients of the services or who are in a position to have special knowledge of the work performed as well as the purposes of the services. Some cautions are in order in this respect. For instance, too often poor communication and the decentralized nature of the school systems result in a serious lack of staff knowledge about many specialist positions. In these types of positions it is necessary to use extra care in the development of job descriptions and objectives to make certain that they are clearly understandable to others.

Also, evaluatees may assume a substantially greater role in the evaluative process, particularly in making self-evaluations and helping prepare job analyses for specialist positions. Aside from all of its conventional benefits, self-evaluation may represent an important area of future refinement in the evaluative process. Sophisticated self-evaluation should permit some telescoping of evaluator time, without losing any of the assessment values.

Evaluation and Management Development

It is not a coincidence that performance evaluation is a keystone in development programs for executives in countless leading corporations. Corporate executives are regarded as valuable investments since a substantial amount of time and money may have been spent in recruiting them and providing them with extensive orientation and in-service training. The challenge for management is to capitalize on the investment—through a systematic in-service effort to develop the skills of executives so that they become increasingly capable of greater achievement in their work assignments. Performance evaluation, with its combination of target setting, counseling, analysis, evaluation, and follow-up, has become a natural and logical component of management development programs.

There may never be a more appropriate time than the present to reemphasize the importance of performance evaluation for public-school administrators and supervisors. Great changes are taking place in terms of complex school organization, decentralized administration, and an upgrading of the positions of administrator and supervisor.

The "management team" is discussed increasingly, although much of the discussion has been the result of militancy on the part of teachers' organizations and the advent of collective bargaining. Too often there is very little genuine understanding in education about the actual meaning of the concept of a management team. Performance evaluation, when properly used in administrative areas, can probably accomplish more toward a better understanding of this concept than all the words and pats on the back that might be offered.

Everything is put into a new perspective when the focus of evaluation is placed upon cooperatively determined performance objectives or targets. Action can be anticipated when well-conceived, work-related goals are the aim of self-effort and supervisory assistance. There is no reason why organizational objectives and individual performance objectives should not mesh, especially if those who determine the targets are members of an administrative team.

Too frequently there are complaints by those in various levels of the managerial hierarchy that communications are inadequate. The superintendent and immediate central-office associates find it difficult to keep closely in touch with administrators who are at the individual school level. This tends to create the "us and them" syndrome—and the gap widens between the central-office and the grass-roots operational units. Face-to-face contacts are too infrequent. Except for the directives and mandates, there is little tangible assurance that there really is a management team. The gap, which widens as a system increases in size and complexity, has serious attitudinal implications that negatively affect performance.

Because of the close contact required between evaluator and evaluatee, performance evaluation helps managerial groups avoid many major communication problems while strengthening the bonds of teamwork. The improved mutual understanding of problems, concerns, aspirations, and expectations that results creates a highly desirable union of the management components.

One of the historic purposes of rating in industry has been to find a proper basis for merit pay. In the evolvement from rating to performance evaluation, some companies have endeavored to retain salary determination as one of the purposes of management personnel evaluation. It is generally difficult to develop an evaluation plan that actually does improve performance and also determines merit increases. Development of such a plan may be even more difficult to achieve in education where salaries often are not confidential, where precise data are lacking to achieve realistic differentiation, and where salary decisions must stand public scrutiny. It is not impossible, however, that the determination of merit pay could be one purpose of evaluation.

The identification of promotable talent, a frequent objective of industry evaluation plans, could well be an objective of an evaluation plan for administrators in education. The availability of evaluator recommendations, based upon comprehensive knowledge and performance information, should give top management far more confidence in its ability to place the proper person in the proper assignment. In addition to providing a systematic way to obtain information regarding promotability, an evaluation plan with this dimension can be useful in counseling administrators and supervisors about the possibilities and probabilities for advancement.

Obviously, any plan that might afford estimates of promotability must be concerned with overall performance as well as with the attainment of performance-related job targets. Most administrator and supervisor evaluation plans do examine over-all performance in terms of administrative and supervisory techniques. No two persons perform administrative and supervisory functions in identical ways; they may get results in different ways. There are fundamental approaches in management methods, however, that can be decisive and are subject to analysis. For example, what do individuals' performances reveal about their ability to delegate? Do they lead or dictate? Do they develop the potentials of their people? What is the quality of their organization and planning? How much skill do they show in carrying out plans and actions?

One of the most significant and valid aspects of the evaluation of principals is a review and study of their evaluation reports of *others* for whom they have been evaluators. In performance evaluation the evaluation summaries made by principals can be most revealing and can help assess many of the leadership qualities they have demonstrated in managing others. A review of evaluations can make any assessment of an administrator's skills far less subjective.

Evaluating General Performance

Performance evaluation of a principal, who may be considered a general administrator, is of great significance. The evaluation of the work of a principal is an evaluation both of general leadership functions and of the specific work that has been assigned to the principalship. As individual schools increase in size as well as offer increasingly complex programs and services, it may be assumed that corresponding arrangements will have to be made for more sophisticated methods of evaluation.

Pressures for specialized school services, course offerings, and programs have demanded the attention of administrators. The more recent and insistent calls for an overall evaluation and the accountability of school districts and individual units, therefore, may represent a healthy and welcome development from the viewpoint of those having administrative responsibilities.

Probably one of the main reasons for the lack of any great enthusiasm on the part of principals for evaluation procedures has been the fact that they have been required to evaluate teachers on the basis of the traditional rating system, which has serious shortcomings. The inadequacy of the traditional system is even more apparent when rating is applied to principals. But principals have been rated and are being rated, often a process without purpose.

On the other hand, performance evaluation of the school principal would increasingly seem to be an imperative. There are certain basic performance areas of the principalship (see Form E). Each performance area—influenced by the goals of the system and of the individual unit—has its own specific goals and objectives for the principalship. In larger schools, the attempt to reach the objectives often involves other members of the school administrative staff as well. In smaller schools, the principal is likely to be the primary performer in seeking to attain each objective.

It may seem trite to include a clear understanding of duties, responsibilities, and job expectations as one of the purposes of evaluation. Yet this understanding may be inadequate as it is often assumed, especially in education, that once individuals are appointed to an administrative or supervisory position they will be able to function satisfactorily without further direction. This gap between assumption and reality, which always has existed, now has widened considerably as the impact of change becomes more intense and wide ranging at the individual school level.

A major purpose in evaluating a principal is to provide assistance in establishing long- and short-term goals and in placing priorities upon those tasks that are the most critical. Also, principals increasingly make their major accomplishments through working with others, and one of the main benefits of evaluation, therefore, is aid in clarifying relationships with others.

Another benefit of evaluation is an improvement in day-by-day operational efficiency. The emphasis upon continual analysis makes it possible to find ways of eliminating purposeless actions and inefficient steps, which have persisted but are undesirable. Finally, the evaluation process makes it possible for a principal to understand better how the quality of his job performance is regarded by those he looks to for advice, counsel, and guidance.

FORM E

RESPONSIBILITY CRITERIA
(For Administrators)

It has been suggested that job content may be defined by responsibility criteria as a substitute for a job description or as a supplement to it. The following criteria are provided to illustrate this approach to job definition.

100 - Organization and Administration

* 101 - Observance of district responsibilities
* 102 - Handling of confidential information
* 103 - Use of research findings
* 104 - Engaging in short- and long-term planning
* 105 - Delegation of responsibility and authority to subordinates
* 106 - Record-keeping practices
* 107 - Accuracy and timeliness of reports
* 108 - Decision-making techniques
* 109 - Holding self accountable for performance
* 110 - Facilitating change
* 111 - Skill in organization
* 112 - Knowledgeability in leadership theory
* 113 - Leadership practices
* 114 - Skill in development of subordinates
  115 - Other (specify)

200 - Communications Management

* 201 - Interpretation of district policies and programs
* 202 - Awareness of concerns and views of the community
* 203 - Responsiveness to inquiries and questions from constituents
* 204 - Keeping colleagues aware of developments in area of responsibility
* 205 - Maintaining open and two-way communication
* 206 - Promoting climate for staff interaction
* 207 - Communication skills
* 208 - Regard for others
* 209 - Participation in district PR programs
  210 - Other (specify)

300 - Personnel Management

* 301 - Participation in employment of personnel
* 302 - Contributions to employee in-service programs
* 303 - Evaluation of personnel for whom responsible
* 304 - Recommendations for additions, promotions, demotions, retentions, transfers, and terminations of personnel
* 305 - Participation in employee relations activities
* 306 - Motivating subordinates
* 307 - Stimulating high morale
* 308 - Orientation of new employees
* 309 - Availability to staff members
* 310 - Sensitivity to needs of staff members
* 311 - Participation in team management
  312 - Other (specify)

400 - Management of Students

  401 - Promotion of health, safety, and welfare of students
  402 - Administration of attendance
  403 - Handling of student behavior problems
  404 - Management of student records
  405 - Observance of rights and responsibilities of students
  406 - Utilization of services of pupil personnel specialists
  407 - Drawing upon resources of community social services
  408 - Administration of district discipline policies and procedures
  409 - Handling of suspensions and expulsions

FORM E, CONTINUED

400 - Management of Students, Continued

      410 - Supervision of extracurricular activities
      411 - Other (specify)

500 - Management of Instruction

    * 501 - Up-to-dateness in curriculum development
    * 502 - Helping to establish systemwide instructional objectives
    * 503 - Facilitation of teaching and learning
    * 504 - Promotion of programs to meet individual differences
    * 505 - Assisting students and teachers to attain instructional
           objectives
    * 506 - Providing resources, materials, supplies, and facilities
           to achieve objectives of instructional program
    * 507 - Building an instructional climate conducive to learning
    * 508 - Using evaluative data to design instructional strategies
    * 509 - Promoting staff development to improve instruction
    * 510 - Performance as a resource person to instructional staff
    * 511 - Participation in the development of instructional goals
    * 512 - Assistance in the evaluation of instructional programs
    * 513 - Monitoring modifications in ongoing instructional operations
      514 - Other (specify)

600 - Management of Services

      601 - Food services program
      602 - Custodial services
      603 - Health care services
      604 - Maintenance services
      605 - Care of school property
      606 - Student transportation
      607 - Safety practices
      608 - Other (specify)

700 - Management of Facilities

    * 701 - Keeping up-to-date inventories
    * 702 - Recommending repairs and replacements of equipment
    * 703 - Identification of new item needs
    * 704 - Adherence to district policies regarding use of school
           facilities
      705 - Contributions to upkeep of buildings and grounds
    * 706 - Care of physical facilities and school property
      707 - Other (specify)

800 - Financial/Business Management

    * 801 - Collection of moneys, maintenance of financial records
    * 802 - Participation in formulation of district budget
    * 803 - Making realistic estimates of financial needs
    * 804 - Adherence to established guidelines governing expenditures
           of funds for goods and services
    * 805 - Observance of cost-effectiveness in budget management
      806 - Other (specify)

900 - Professional Competencies and Improvement

    * 901 - Sensitivity to need to grow professionally
    * 902 - Up-to-dateness in area(s) of specialization
    * 903 - Participation in additional graduate training
    * 904 - Participation in development activities
    * 905 - Contributions to districtwide in-service training activities
    * 906 - Allocation of time to professional development
      907 - Other (specify)

Notes: All descriptors marked (*) are believed applicable to central-
office specialists as well as building-level persons.

Items marked "Other" provide opportunity to add descriptors not
included in the various areas.

General Principles of Evaluation

Self-evaluation, as suggested previously, is every bit as important for the administrator or supervisor as for anyone else in a performance review. In some cases, self-evaluation may best be conducted without assistance from others; in others, because of the many dimensions of the situation, evaluatees may prefer to have some assistance from people on their administrative team.

Perhaps one of the great weaknesses in management has been to link evaluation to the calendar and to regard this function as having its greatest value as an annual event. On the contrary, evaluation produces the best results when it provides evaluatees with information about their performance more often than once a year. Quarterly reports are sometimes recommended, but this presumes that the number of evaluatees an evaluator must evaluate is reasonably small. In most school systems the number of evaluation reports is more likely to be two per year. The value of having at least a midyear assessment, in addition to the one at the end of the year, is to provide additional time to make necessary adjustments that may enable the evaluatee to be more successful.

Success depends heavily upon being success oriented. This is exemplified in performance evaluation by the careful attention and emphasis given to the setting of performance objectives or job targets. In order to maintain the success orientation, it is necessary to monitor performance data and to utilize it to maximum advantage year-round to achieve success rather than to store the data away to be used only at the end of an evaluation period. It is just as important, if not more so, to be able to capitalize upon information for an upward adjustment of sights as it is to acquire data for the purpose of trying to avoid failure.

In a sense, principals can be said to be involved in self-evaluation when they and their staff members study performance data on a continuing basis. The information may be of some help in making the overall evaluation at a later date, but the feedback and immediate use of data can positively affect target achievement.

Typically, the primary evaluators of principals are their

superiors. Over the years many experimental patterns have been attempted by management-development people in industry and by merit-pay raters. These experiments have involved a variety of committee and panel arrangements, most of which represented efforts to guard against individual bias in rating. The more recent emergence of management by objectives and performance evaluation has caused less emphasis to be placed upon large numbers of coevaluators.

The patterns now in use, however, do frequently involve the use of primary and contributing evaluators as well as evaluation reviewers. The reviewer, frequently the superior of the primary evaluator, may receive the evaluator's tentative estimates of accomplishment. The reviewer checks over the evaluation estimate and responds in writing to the evaluator, who then finalizes the evaluation. In other arrangements, the evaluator may confer with others who are familiar with the evaluatee's work. They review the job targets and progress made. The evaluator then prepares the evaluation.

It is not uncommon, at meetings where a proposed evaluation is discussed, to include someone who is a specialist in the techniques of the performance evaluation plan as it has been designed for the particular company or institution. The specialist's function is to make certain that the plan and the procedures are carried out correctly. The specialist is not involved in making any contributions to the evaluations involved, only to the process.

Under ideal circumstances, a performance evaluation program might best be launched initially at the administrative and supervisory levels simply to permit those individuals to acquire the skills needed for successful evaluation. Since the bulk of the administrator-supervisor group will eventually become evaluators of others, beginning the evaluation program at the managerial level carries special significance. Evaluators who have had prior experience with the process, at least as evaluatees, are likely to carry out their responsibilities without serious bungling.

One of the greatest points of vulnerability of performance evaluation in public education has been the failure by a large majority of educators to properly estimate the amount of orientation and training needed. The mechanics of performance evaluation are fairly simple to grasp, but implementation frequently is deceptively difficult.

Performance evaluation actually involves a radical change in the basis for managing most school districts. The nature of supervision is altered drastically, and the subordinate-superior relationship is placed in a new dimension. Above all, performance evaluation is completely different from conventional rating, except for superficial outward similarities. Thus, those who embark upon a program of performance evaluation also must recognize that they probably have made the most ambitious in-service training commitment that has ever been undertaken in their school or school district.

It can be disastrous to underestimate the training that is necessary. Misunderstandings and naiveté, as well as ineptness in carrying out any stage of the evaluation process, can lead to serious trouble. The leadership group that recognizes this pitfall and avoids it is the one that will eventually reap the tremendous positive benefits for all that are inherent in a soundly developed and implemented performance evaluation program.

Specifics of Evaluation

Defining the Job

There are various ways to define the jobs of administrators and supervisors, and one method, to use responsibility criteria, has been suggested. Duties and responsibilities should be defined in writing regardless of the format used. This is the initial step in the evaluation process. If it is decided to use the criteria-and-descriptor format, certain advantages will become apparent.

1. Duties classified into broad categories, with descriptors under each, have the advantage of being both explicit and comprehensive in scope. By providing open-ended items under each category, it is possible to provide for unique and specialized work requirements.
2. The numbering system for both major categories and clarifying descriptors facilitates their use in subsequent steps of the evaluation process.
3. Needs or areas in which improvement should be undertaken can be identified more readily by means of the numbering system.
4. When it comes time to complete summative assessments,

the numbered descriptors make it possible to cite areas where commendation is due and those where additional improvement should be undertaken.

The entire evaluation process will go better if the job definition phase is carefully done.

Identifying Needs

A prerequisite for establishing useful performance objectives is a process for identifying areas in the list of responsibility criteria that should be strengthened. Evaluatees should analyze their current strengths and weaknesses in relation to the criteria. Given the expectations of the job, the evaluatee and the evaluator cooperatively determine what needs to be done to enable the former to improve certain aspects of overall performance. This inventory becomes the basis for developing performance objectives.

Performance Objectives

Objectives should be written in concrete terms and, to the extent possible, should be stated in behavioral terms. Three questions should be considered in writing an objective: (a) Is it stated in concise terms? (b) Is the desired outcome clearly indicated? and (c) Is the method of measurement stated? Insofar as possible, desired outcomes should be expressed in terms of results that are amenable to some form of measurement rather than to opinion or guesswork.

Desired outcomes may be limited by constraints over which the evaluatee has little or no control. While objectives ought to be challenging, at the same time they need to be realistic. It is foolish to propose objectives that have little possibility of being achieved. This does not mean, however, that they should be so undemanding or irrelevant that they can be achieved with little or no effort. Setting easy, self-fulfilling objectives is game playing in the evaluation process.

Action Plans

A plan of action has two aspects: the specific actions to be taken to attain the objective and an understanding of the ways the evaluatee and the evaluator will work together in carrying out the action plan. For each action plan, agreement should be reached regarding the

> Kinds and amount of evaluator assistance that will be provided
> Extent of observational or other contacts that the evaluator will make with the evaluatee
> Frequency of follow-up, feedback conferences
> Kinds of evaluative data that will be collected and used in the making of assessments

An important guideline to follow is that "there shall be no surprises" during the evaluation process. In other words, this means close working contacts between the evaluatee and the evaluator throughout each phase of the process. The nature of the objectives will determine the type and extent of these contacts.

Generally speaking, the major responsibility for implementing an action plan rests with the evaluatee. The evaluator serves best in the roles of reviewer and ultimate rater of the evaluatee's effectiveness.

Assessing Results

Assessments of results should occur at least twice a year. One should take place about the midpoint of the evaluation year; the other at the end of the year. The midpoint assessment should ascertain how things are going and whether sufficient progress is being made. The end-of-the-year assessment should make bottom-line evaluations both on the attainment of objectives and on the degree of overall performance.

Assessments are made by the primary evaluator, usually the individual's immediate supervisor. Supplemental information may be obtained from others who are in a position to make responsible judgments about the evaluatee's work.

Discussing Results

A follow-up conference should occur after each written assessment is completed, midpoint and summative. The conference following the summative evaluation is the occasion to discuss implications of the assessments and to do preliminary planning for the next evaluation cycle.

It is important to consider the human consequences of evaluation. The process does set certain feedback procedures into motion, and it must be remembered that evaluation is a sensitive process. Damage can be done unless certain cautions are exercised. First, the temptation to design a comprehensive evaluation program calculated to accomplish every purpose the school system seeks to achieve should be resisted. For example, one program to promote improvement and professional growth, to make personnel decisions with reference to retention, transfer, or termination, and to determine salary tries to do too much. The purposes are diverse and, to some extent, in conflict. To expect one program of evaluation to achieve all of these purposes may turn out to be an unrealistic expectation.

Second, in using evaluation as a tool for consultation with administrators and supervisors, it should be recognized that different approaches will have to be used with different persons. "Zero-sum" comparisons should be avoided. Third, avoid using a closed-system evaluation program; evaluation should be open ended and future oriented.

School administrators are well advised to recognize the gap that may exist between good intentions and desired results. Those who design the evaluation program may feel it is fair and useful. They may find, however, that the program produces discouragement, cynicism, and alienation on the part of those being evaluated.

The impetus for instituting or revising an evaluation program should come from the highest level. The superintendent must believe in the idea, and the board of education should understand what such a program is designed to accomplish and be willing to give it policy-level support from both a philosophical and a financial point of view. Given this support, it will stand a good chance of success.

5

Evaluating Substandard Performance

The steps in the evaluation process for those whose performance is regarded as being unsatisfactory are essentially the same as for all other evaluatees. There are, however, some particular emphases that are different. Whenever it becomes apparent that the services of an individual are less than satisfactory, concentrated efforts must be made to help the person correct what is wrong. The length of time required to do this will be determined by the nature and severity of the problems.

Deficiencies must be carefully, completely, and explicitly defined, and evidence of each deficiency has to be stated in writing. Steps to be taken to correct each deficiency must be clearly stated. The individual should be invited to request specific kinds and amounts of assistance, and such requests must be honored, to the extent the school system has the capacity to do so. The assistance must be timely.

All observations needed must be made, and follow-up reports should be prompt and pay particular attention to the recommendations. Follow-up conferences need to be held promptly also. It is assumed that the individual whose performance is considered unsatisfactory and the evaluator will work in a cooperative way throughout the evaluation process to help the former overcome deficiencies and perform duties satisfactorily.

Complete and careful records of all assistance given and all contacts made must be kept with copies of each given to the individual. Summative assessments must reflect all performance data collected during the year. All recommendations on the Summative Evaluation Report must be substantiated with appropriate backup data. If the ultimate decision is to recommend nonrenewal of contract, all steps required by due process must have been completed properly.

A persistent admonition of many superintendents and school board members is to be certain that the evaluation program will positively identify so-called deadwood so that it can be eliminated. This is an oversimplification of a complex process. There is no doubt that the evaluation program should be reliably effective in dealing with those whose work falls below the satisfactory level. The way the process is carried out, however, is exceedingly important.

The first obligation is to identify explicitly the nature of the deficiencies and to prescribe appropriate corrective remedies. Remediation requires adequate and accurate information, usually gathered by means of increased observations and other contacts with the individual, so that the evaluator will be fully informed about the nature of the deficiencies. Supervision has to be more intensive and assistance more responsive and appropriate to the needs of the person. All contacts between the parties have to be carefully and conscientiously documented.

This kind of careful attention, given to those who are experiencing difficulties in performing their duties, will usually help them improve sufficiently to become satisfactory in the performance of their work. In some instances, however, the improvement may not be sufficient. If the prognosis still remains doubtful after ample time and effort have been expended in applying remediation, so that nonrenewal of contract or termination is justified, the documented evidence must be sufficient in scope and substance to justify the recommended action. Before deciding to recommend termination, however, it is advisable to check with legal counsel to make sure that all requirements have been observed and that there is sufficient evidence to justify a recommendation to discharge the individual. Failure to take this precaution often results in difficulty because some important procedure may have been overlooked.

It is important to emphasize that the percentage of persons considered to be performing below the satisfactory level is likely to be relatively small—perhaps only 5 to 10 percent. It should also be pointed out that if good employment practices are observed by a school system, only a small number of persons will have to be terminated because of sustained and demonstrated deficiencies.

It is sometimes suggested that there should be two different kinds of evaluation programs, one for individuals who perform their duties successfully and another for those who do not. Such a dichotomy is not necessary; the same type of process will work for both groups with some differences in application of the procedures. For those who are not performing well, it is necessary to be sure that (a) deficiencies are identified as early as possible and with as much precision as can be applied, (b) prescribed remediation is detailed and concrete, (c) supervision is directed toward correcting the deficiencies, (d) assistance is greater in quantity and quality, (e) observations and all other contacts are detailed and fully documented, and (f) all rights granted by due process are fully and faithfully observed.

For those whose job performance is satisfactory, the emphasis should be upon further professional growth and development. Successful people usually are able to take more initiative in this regard, carry out their plans more independently, and hold themselves more strictly accountable for the achievement of challenging objectives.

The evaluation program should serve both groups. Competent people should be motivated to become even more effective, and those who are in difficulty should be helped so that deficiencies can be corrected and satisfactory status may be attained. If some are still unable to do their jobs satisfactorily after help has been given, the evaluation process must provide the kind and quality of evidence and information needed to substantiate recommendations for termination of services.

Details of Procedure

Step 1: Identify Specific Deficiencies. This is the responsibility of the evaluator who measures current performance against responsibility criteria. This analysis is supplemented by classroom and/or work-station observations, the number of which will depend upon the severity of the deficiencies.

Step 2: The Evaluatee and Evaluator Confer. The purpose of this conference is to clarify the nature of the deficiencies. The evaluator presents the evaluatee with a written prescription indicating (a) the areas in which the evaluatee is deficient, (b) recommendations for corrective action, (c) the kinds and sources of assistance that will be made available, (d) a suggested time schedule for correcting the deficiencies, and (e) observational and other contacts that will take place.

Step 3: Fulfill the Prescribed Improvement Plan. This is a dual responsibility of the evaluatee and the evaluator. The latter provides more intensive supervision, conducts frequent observations, and promptly provides feedback so that the evaluatee may know the evaluator's views about the progress being made. Full documentation of all the contacts is exceedingly important in case it ultimately becomes necessary to recommend some kind of terminating action.

Step 4: Assess Results. The extent to which specific difficulties have been overcome composes one part of the summary assessment process. The evaluation of overall performance, with reference to the responsibility criteria, is the other part of the summary assessment.

Step 5: Confer Regarding Results. If sufficient improvement has occurred, the conference should not be difficult. Tenseness in these types of conferences usually can be reduced if the evaluator makes constructive suggestions that the evaluatee may be able to adopt to bring about necessary improvements. This puts criticism in a more positive context and changes the tone of the conference. If enough improvement has not taken place, this conference can be a traumatic experience for both parties. It is absolutely essential for the evaluator to make careful preparation for the conference and to have everything in good order. The evaluatee is likely to be upset, and when one's job is in jeopardy, it is natural to be defensive and seek ways to refute an evaluator's assessments. It is advisable, in difficult summative conferences, to stick to the facts and avoid getting bogged down in personality clashes. Good conference techniques can be taught, but skill in conducting such conferences comes from both training and experience. *What* is done in working with those who are performing poorly is important, but *how* it is done is even more important. The approach makes the difference.

The suggestions made in this chapter are based upon the following assumptions.

• Individuals can improve their performance unless they are hopelessly incompetent. Improvement and growth are possibilities throughout one's career.

• One of the most useful functions of the evaluator is to assist in the improvement of performance. This may mean an evaluator must learn to shift from merely judging and rating toward more coaching and expediting.

• Assessing results achieved is more productive than evaluating efforts expended. The bottom line should be achievement, which definitely produces improvement.

• Equally important is the evaluation of overall performance in relation to predetermined responsibility criteria. Specific improvement may be restricted to definite areas of need, but it is necessary to have an estimate of how well the individual is doing overall.

• A primary evaluator must be held responsible for making the summative assessment of overall performance as well as for judging the extent to which improvement has occurred in specific areas of need. Other people may serve in contributing roles, but the ultimate responsibility belongs to the primary evaluator.

• Contributors to the evaluation process may be department heads, team leaders, consultants, and central-office specialists.

• By mutual consent of the evaluatee and evaluator, suggestions and advisement from clients may be used in evaluation. Students may be considered clients of teachers; teachers, the clients of principals; and principals, the clients of central-office personnel.

• A method for resolving differences between evaluatee and evaluator should be developed. While it may seldom be used, it serves as insurance for those occasions when disputes do arise.

• An understanding of people and skill in working with them are important in working with those individuals who may be having difficulty doing their work well. The quality of working relationships can make a great difference in carrying out the evaluation procedures.

These premises may seem to suggest a commitment to a soft

approach in evaluation. This is not the intent. They do constitute the essential ingredients in a positive type of evaluation, which is essential in working with both successful and less able individuals.

Some Advice for Evaluating Substandard Work

Incompetence. Be careful about using the general term "incompetence" as the basis for recommending nonrenewal or termination of contract. Incompetence is difficult to prove. It requires an evaluation that is free of error, both procedurally and substantively. This is not to say that an attempt to prove incompetence should never be undertaken, but generally it is wiser to define specific deficiencies and use evaluation records to show that they have or have not been corrected.

Advisement. It is useful to get advice from the superintendent (or a designee) at the outset of, during the course of, and at the culmination of the evaluation process for an individual who is not performing well. If some sort of termination action may become necessary, the top administrators must be well informed about each step along the way. Consultation with counsel is likewise necessary to be sure that legal errors are avoided.

Time. It requires a great deal of time to work with those whose performance is below standard. There is no such thing as a "quick fix" in performance evaluation. This means that evaluators will have to allocate a double, triple, or even quadruple amount of time to do a thorough job with those whose work is substandard.

Thoroughness. Slipshod, superficial, inadequate evaluative actions won't do. In fact, they will make a travesty of the evaluation process, especially in the case of those individuals who are performing below acceptable levels.

Documentation. The bottom line in evaluating substandard performance is to have complete records of all observations, follow-up conferences, assistance provided, actions of the evaluatee, and all other contacts between evaluatee and evaluator.

Comparability. There is a possibility that by treating those whose performance is substandard differently from those whose work is quite satisfactory, a charge of a lack of comparability may be made. In other words, presumably all people have to be evaluated similarly. The response to such an allegation is that (a) the same evaluation process *is* being used for all evaluatees, (b) the difference lies in application only, (c) all those having serious problems are treated in the same way, and (d) likewise, all those who are performing well are evaluated in the same manner. The point to be made is that the comparability principle is not being violated. The needs of individuals differ; therefore the application of the evaluation procedures has to be adjusted accordingly in order to serve well the needs of those whose work is substandard as well as those whose work is satisfactory.

Harassment. It is also possible that an individual whose work is substandard may charge the school system, and especially the primary evaluator, with harassment because the evaluation process has been applied more intensely and with greater initiative on the part of the evaluator in his case than it has in others. The best answer to this possible charge is to make sure that each of the steps described earlier is completed properly and with objectivity. As long as the evaluator and others involved in the process maintain poise, impartiality, and objectivity in all of their contacts with the evaluatee, any charge of harassment will prove baseless.

Legalities. The value of getting advice from legal counsel has already been emphasized. While this is very important and necessary, advice is one thing; dictation is quite another matter. Sometimes evaluators sacrifice some humane considerations in carrying out the evaluation process so that the work of legal counsel will be facilitated if termination becomes a reality. There need be no serious conflict between carrying out the evaluation process properly, and humanely, and adhering to necessary legal requirements.

Danger in Predetermining Termination. Care must be exercised to avoid the charge that school officials decide, in advance, to terminate an individual and that evaluation is merely a pro forma exercise. In other words, evaluation actions are designed and carried out to "complete the book" on an individual. It is absolutely necessary to start out with the assumption that the first priority is to help an individual's job performance become satisfactory. The emphasis must be upon remediation of deficiencies. Only after it is clearly demonstrated that the deficiencies haven't been corrected and that the prognosis for improvement is clearly negative is it time to assemble the data necessary to justify a recommendation for termination.

6

The Principal's New Role

Evaluation by objectives casts the principal in a quite different role than in the traditional rating type of evaluation. Inspectional contacts with teachers are deemphasized; partnership interactions are greatly increased. So changed is the role of the principal that one of the critical aspects is to gain an understanding of the full implications involved. Those principals who have participated in traditional modes of rating and supervision frequently have some difficulty in clearly visualizing how performance evaluation alters relationships and conditions. Perhaps one of the confusing aspects is that some of the highly visible procedures are similar under traditional rating systems and evaluation by objectives.

The traditional teacher-principal three-step sequence of rating is observation, evaluation, and conference. Underlying this procedure are quite a few assumptions, which may or may not be true, that are subscribed to by those who believe that traditional rating is effective. It is presumed that the teacher is the chief planner and implementer of the instructional process and that the principal plays a secondary role—he observes, assesses, and advises. It is presumed also that observations will provide enough information to accurately judge the quality of instruction and, further, that the principal has enough expertise to make a valid evaluation. Finally, it is assumed that both are able to communicate fully and with complete understanding throughout the procedure and that the teacher readily accepts the evaluator's assessment.

Undoubtedly, there have been many instances over the years

where traditional rating has seemed to operate satisfactorily. Too many of the assumptions, however, do not always conform to reality. In these days of complex organizations, innovative practices, expansion of knowledge, and new developments, it becomes increasingly difficult for a principal to achieve or maintain an across-the-board expertise in instruction. The situation becomes more unrealistic when it is recognized that instructional supervision is only one of a number of basic administrative duties of the contemporary principal. If this is the situation, how can principals become more effective instructional directors? The answer lies in changing the fundamental evaluation relationship between teachers and principals.

Supervision and Evaluation

The essence of more competent evaluation is to combine supervision and assessment—to move away from inspectional observation and to avoid a unilateral rating of teaching performance. Rather than attempt to estimate the relative quality of competence solely on the basis of classroom observations, a more productive approach is for the principal and teacher to

> Agree upon specific performance objectives after having made an inventory of needs to ascertain those things that should be done to improve performance
> Establish ways and means to check periodically on the extent to which daily instructional procedures are achieving desired results
> Make cooperative, evaluative estimates of results attained
> Confer as to the implications of the assessments made by both the teacher and the principal

This is a type of teacher-principal interaction that puts a high priority upon joint instructional planning, cooperative implementing effort, and a shared review of results. The key words are planning, implementing, and reviewing. If instructional improvement is the chief objective, this process makes more sense than a unilateral evaluation wherein the principal attempts to assess teaching effectiveness in the traditional manner.

Experience in business and industrial circles has yielded much useful information about evaluatee-evaluator relationships that also applies to teachers and principals. Aspects of the evaluation process that have been studied include some of the following: (a) attitudes of evaluatee and evaluator toward evaluation, (b) extent to which the former truly wants to know how his work is regarded, (c) the impact of feedback about the quality of work performance upon the correction of performance deficiencies.

Much to the dismay of many, the evidence seems to show that even though both evaluatee and evaluator profess faith in evaluation by objectives, neither party is completely eager to get on with the process, nor is either party always enthusiastic about the interaction requirement of the evaluation procedure. To paraphrase a slogan, evaluation by objectives makes people work more closely together, but they may seem to enjoy it less and less. Why this paradox?

Some of the lessons learned in the business and industrial settings may well prevent principals from making the same mistakes in performance evaluation. Translated into the realm of education, these lessons learned include the following:

> Beware of too much criticism. A criticism overload has a negative effect upon the attainment of performance objectives.
>
> Don't count on praise to make every teacher feel "nine feet tall." Praise may or may not promote improvement. Recognition probably is a more potent force than praise, particularly if the latter is superficial.
>
> Improvement gains are greatest when performance objectives are specific. Clear, explicit work objectives, which have the capability of being assessed with a reasonable degree of objectivity, offer the greatest opportunity for increasing teacher effectiveness.
>
> Continuing teacher-principal contacts are preferable to one year-end conference to discuss the year's work.
>
> Blending personal and school system objectives is more productive than overemphasizing one to the exclusion of the other.

Teacher participation in goal setting for the individual
school and for the system as a whole contributes to a
sense of personal development and professional growth.

Employ a Variety of Approaches

There are many ways for principals to work with teachers.
Relationships are also infinitely varying. The principal can say
one thing to Teacher A that may be very inappropriate for
Teacher B. One may accept gratefully what another may angrily
reject. The principal must become especially sensitive to the
nuances of personalities.

Beginning teachers usually want and welcome concrete suggestions, precise directions, and strong supervisory guidance
when performance objectives are being considered. Experienced
teachers, even though they may be unfamiliar with performance evaluation procedures, do not usually need or want
the principal to be overly assertive when their objectives are
being formulated.

Teachers are most likely to welcome constructive advice
and help when the principal genuinely wants to be helpful and
is able to give the time and energy required. Students of the
evaluation process make much of the terms "mutual trust"
and "sincerity," carefully underlining the kind of relationship
that makes for the best rapport. Fair and even unflattering
comments can be made when the relationship between the
evaluatee and the evaluator is one of genuine friendship and
trust. Conversely, a steady flow of effusive praise may not indicate real interest. To use another term, a "climate of acceptance"
must exist between teacher and principal.

One of the skills most needed by a principal to develop good
working relationships with teachers is to be able to listen. To
listen patiently and intently is an essential art of the executive.
Sometimes an overdynamic, self-assertive principal, although
highly regarded by his superiors, may be quite ineffective in the
interaction required by the evaluation process. This does not
mean that principals should become nondirective counselors.
The goal to strive for is shared participation at each stage of the
evaluation process.

Develop Sensitive Radar

It is essential to be aware of the problems and concerns of teachers. Awareness and a timely response may prevent a progression into acute difficulties. Especially in large, complicated school systems, teachers cannot solve all their problems without help from the principal. He has to cut red tape, remove roadblocks, and facilitate the teacher's work.

New teachers face many adjustment problems, and the principal must have time to make himself aware of these and give help. Providing a "listening post" when assistance is needed is a responsibility of major proportions. Operational difficulties abound in most school systems, and teachers tend to hesitate to ask for help because they sometimes think this might be regarded as a sign of weakness. Principals must be sensitive to this possibility and make asking for help a nonthreatening act. All impediments to good teaching performance cannot be eliminated, but the effective administrator removes as many as possible.

Changing Relationships

In the evolvement of school management, relationships between teachers and principals have changed sharply in recent years. Many long-established and cherished beliefs about the principalship are under fire. The principal as a planner, director, and evaluator is under challenge; so is his role as instructional leader.

In many ways, collective bargaining has made the teacher-principal relationship into a "new ball game." The teacher liberation movement predates other liberation movements by several years. Paternalism has been rejected. The adversary climate generated by negotiations between teachers and boards of education often spills over into local schools. Principals can find themselves isolated as teachers are persuaded to perceive them as adversaries. Hard feelings spawned at the bargaining table can filter into the day-to-day working relationships between teachers and principals. Admittedly this development complicates relationships in the evaluation process. On the other hand, performance evaluation can strengthen the professional relationship between teachers and principals in a way that is highly beneficial to both.

Every effort must be made to separate bargaining from supervision and evaluation. At all costs, rigidities that will impede or stifle cooperative working relationships so vital in evaluation by objectives should not be negotiated into contracts.

Human Relations Emphasis

Advocates of good human relations between teachers and principals believe that emphasis on a human relations program will serve as an antidote for deteriorating relationships caused, in large part, by collective bargaining and the growth and complexity of the schools of today. Proponents of better human relations in teacher-principal interactions believe that teachers should (1) be more responsibly involved in school management, not as a negotiated privilege but as an inherent right; (2) share in decision making in those areas where their expertise and experience may improve the quality of the decision; (3) become a part of the total program of the school and not be completely preoccupied by one aspect of the program; and (4) derive from their work personal and professional satisfaction, recognition, and a sense of being valued as important contributors to the total educational enterprise.

Basic to the concept of good human relations is the assumption that when teachers genuinely feel involved, are consulted, and become identified with overall operational policies and procedures, they will gain the intrinsic satisfaction so essential to successful performance.

Capitalize on Staff Resources

Good human relations are essential, but further administrative efforts are necessary in order to unlock creativity and to produce maximum performance effectiveness. That "extra something" is to regard the individual as a human resource. In more specific terms, it means that effective teachers

> Have needs beyond desiring to belong, to be appreciated, or to be respected. They want to make contributions

that only they can make. In so doing they become a human resource in the educational process.

Need more than a feeling of usefulness. They have untapped capacities to initiate actions, to take on greater levels of responsibility, and to display creativity far in excess of what they customarily display.

Should be able to amplify their skills and talents while accomplishing their own objectives as well as those of their schools.

Should be able to expand their capabilities for self-direction and self-control.

Can and should have the opportunity to exercise a higher level of self-direction and responsibility. This is more likely to occur when they have a full partnership in the establishment of the objectives of the school in which they work and of the system as a whole.

Principal as Evaluator

In a fuller leadership sense, principals are personnel managers. As such, they should perfect their special skills in personnel management because those skills are essential in carrying out the evaluation process. The first step is to recognize the importance of personnel management skills, and principals should then analyze critically the personnel procedures used in their schools.

The ramifications of positive and negative practices in personnel management are both extensive and clear, and principals must perfect their knowledge and skills in this area if they are to adequately fulfill their roles as supervisors and evaluators. There is no simple test available to the principal to ascertain his competence in personnel management. The best approach is through self-analysis and a deliberate effort to enhance one's personnel skills. There are some key areas, however, that are worth particular attention.

Leadership Characteristics

Principals must continually ask themselves if their actions affect teachers positively or negatively. They must keep their own motivations and drives under scrutiny. Insight is important to a healthy outlook, an important ingredient in productive leadership. Principals have to accept themselves if they expect teachers to accept them. Being able to look within, to search out motives, and to treat others as they would wish to be treated are aspects of insight.

Principals, like all others, need a sense of personal security. The devastating effects of deep personal insecurities show up in leadership behavior, and they are very detrimental to good working relationships with teachers. Personal insecurity may manifest itself in punitive type actions, overdomination, self-justification, erratic behavior, and various other forms of ineffective leadership action. The cure is to increase one's sense of personal security.

As the principal's responsibilities become more complex and difficult, there is a tendency to become insensitive and arbitrary. The best insurance against dictatorial behavior is self-discipline and a strong determination to care about the feelings of others. Sensitivity is vital and must be consistently cultivated.

The principal who operates on the basis of whim or expediency is engaging in potentially dangerous behavior. Decision on the basis of intuition is risky and means that too often the symptoms of problems and not their causes are treated. A consistent practice of diagnosing objectively and rationally the causes of problems is one characteristic of maturity in leadership.

Leadership responsibilities are neither simple nor static. The principal, to function effectively, is obliged to operate within a flexible framework. Tactics and procedures must fit the exigencies of the day. However, flexibility must not be confused with ambivalence. A well-defined thread of consistency must run through leadership actions.

Personal Fulfillment

Principals' jobs are becoming increasingly demanding. To be equal to the demands, principals must gain as much personal satisfaction as possible from their tasks and responsibilities. The traditional evaluation process has not been a pathway to this kind of realization, but evaluation by objectives, in that it stresses affirmative relationships and positive action, has a great potential for generating personal fulfillment. This applies not only to evaluatees but also to principals. As they are able to help teachers establish worthwhile objectives, expedite their accomplishment, and share in the successes of performance, principals can gain intrinsic satisfaction from their work.

Evaluation by objectives is closely related to the concept of intrinsic motivation. Most people receive the greatest satisfaction and sense of accomplishment from job achievement, responsibility, growth, and earned recognition. These are the areas in which performance objectives are likely to be formed. The degree to which principals understand the significance of the intrinsic motivation theory (as they work with teachers in evaluation) affects how well they attain the most positive results for teachers—and for themselves.

Other Roles of the Principal

As presently organized, the principalship requires that an inordinate amount of time and attention be spent on administrative duties that often do not appear to bear directly upon instructional improvement and performance evaluation. Public relations problems, crisis resolution, student behavior, negotiated-contract administration, and other tension-laden problems are recognized parts of principals' jobs. They find themselves shorthanded and overloaded with administrative detail.

Because of these demands, it is valid to question whether or not the principal can possibly devote enough time to instructional leadership and performance analysis as is called for in evaluation by objectives. An early task, therefore, is to decide how directly the principal can realistically be involved as a supervisor and an evaluator. In many instances, substantial adjustments will have to be made in his duties and responsibilities in order for him to fulfill those roles.

The board of education and the superintendent will have to want those changes and take the initiative in making the modifications. Many boards and superintendents may not favor making the changes. If not, the principal's role in evaluation will have to be altered from that of prime evaluator to a role less demanding of time and involvement. There are several possible alternatives.

Serve as Reviewer

When this alternative is used, the teachers work directly with department heads, the head teacher, and instructional supervisors when making the needs assessments and forming performance objectives. The principal reviews the objectives and directly assists teachers as time permits. Most of the supervisory assistance comes through the same persons (department heads, instructional supervisors, and consultants) who normally provide supervisory assistance. But assessment of performance objectives is also performed by these individuals, and the principal reviews the assessments. He appends his evaluation of each teacher by endorsing the teacher's self-evaluation and that of the supervisor or by adding his own assessments.

This type of approach may not be as easy as it sounds. In many instances school systems, especially smaller ones, do not provide supervisory services to teachers. If department heads are not used in this manner, only the principal is available to serve as supervisor and evaluator. This makes the reviewer role impossible, of course. In such a situation and if the principal is not given time to properly function as a full-fledged evaluator, he is forced to operate in a very superficial manner, which is unfair to all involved. In fact, it is pretense and debases good management. Another handicap of the reviewer approach is that supervisory personnel may object to being used as evaluators because they may fear that that role will endanger their working relationships with teachers.

Faced with these impediments, it can be exceedingly difficult to implement a comprehensive program of evaluation by objectives in which the principal acts as reviewer only.

Limit Evaluation Scope

Assuming that the overwhelming percentage of teachers perform well above the satisfactory level, it might be possible to delegate to supervisory personnel (supervisors, heads of departments, head teachers, etc.) the responsibility for evaluating those deemed to be in the "satisfactory" category. The principal would work with and evaluate teachers whose performance is substandard. This approach would help satisfy the frequent assertion by teachers' organizations that evaluation is a task the teaching profession itself is capable of carrying out and should be allowed to carry out.

If this approach is implemented, certain understandings have to be reached between teachers and school administrators. Both parties have to pursue the goals and mission of the school system with equal vigor, and both have to be committed to using evaluation as a vehicle to promote improvement of professional services. Teachers have to be willing to assume the responsibility for setting rigorous performance objectives, work diligently to attain them, and be steadfast in assessing results fairly and accurately. Furthermore, teachers have to organize themselves to carry out the evaluation process. Departmental objectives have to be established, and various organizational arrangements have to be developed to make collegial evaluation feasible and workable.

If principals restrict themselves to the evaluation of teachers performing below the satisfactory level, their evaluatee-evaluator ratio will probably be reduced sufficiently to enable them to carry out the function without a major modification of their other duties and responsibilities. One obvious difficulty with principals evaluating only the marginal and unsatisfactory teachers is that principals probably will dislike the role. They might feel they would be regarded as "black hat" adversaries and their supervisory counterparts would be regarded as "white hat" advocates.

The most difficult consideration, of course, is whether teachers will or can assume such a major role in an evaluation program based upon performance objectives. Those teachers who are also evaluators are required to be more directly accountable to the school board, parents, and public, which can become uncomfortable and burdensome.

It is also possible to cycle evaluations in a way that will reduce the principal's number of evaluatees. Experienced teachers, whose performance is demonstrated as being satisfactory, may be evaluated only in alternate years or every third year. This would leave new staff members and those whose work is below par to be evaluated annually, reducing the evaluation load of principals.

There is a negative aspect to this approach, however. One of the major purposes of performance evaluation is the positive impact on performance made possible by a closer understanding and communication between principal and teacher. When the cycle is limited to every second or third year, much of the improvement aspect may be dissipated.

Delegate Some Evaluation Responsibilities

In those instances where principals have assistants, another possibility may be to use assistant principals as evaluators. It is sometimes argued that teachers are reluctant to be evaluated by anyone except the principal, but this is not an insurmountable problem. Assistant principals can be trained to fulfill the evaluation function, and teachers may see that it is in their best interests to benefit from a reasonable evaluatee-evaluator ratio. The decisive factor may be that a performance evaluation system can be used rather than the traditional rating system, which means the teacher will have a major role in the process.

A major weakness of evaluation-by-committee arrangements is the dilution of the partnership factor. This includes the inability of a committee to adequately play the role of coach, to effectively interact and communicate with the evaluatee, or to be accountable for its actions—or lack of actions—in providing and upholding management commitments to help a teacher achieve job targets. The jurylike personality of a committee also may cause it to unintentionally direct its efforts simply to passing judgment upon those evaluated. In other words, the ultimate result of an elaborate committee structure might actually be that several persons, with diffused accountability, do old-fashioned teacher rating—rating that formerly was done by one accountable person. This scarcely is progress.

Experimental efforts to involve others than the principal in the evaluation procedure should not be ruled out however. There may be other new ways to overcome the serious organizational handicaps that have been imposed upon the principalship in larger units of most school systems.

Coaching Role

The important point to remember is that there is no one best role for the principal in the evaluation process. Each school system must define the principal's role as circumstances dictate. If the role has to be that of prime evaluator, the decks will have to be cleared to make that feasible. Should it be possible to make the evaluation role a secondary one there should be no hesitancy in trying one of the alternative approaches. However, in all probability, the principal must assume final responsibility for summative evaluation statements, whether they result from his direct assessments or from the judgments of those to whom he has delegated the task.

While each principal must determine which role he can best fulfill as an evaluator, there is one type of role each is advised to consider carefully, the "coaching" role. The principal becomes a diagnostician, counselor, motivator, expediter, and helper, all of which are facets of the coaching role. As improvement is the object of the evaluation process, the teacher and the evaluator stand to gain if their efforts are productive, and they must accept shared responsibility for failure to attain some objectives. They are partners rather than evaluator and evaluatee, a significant difference.

The coaching responsibility is compatible with the supervisory role that facilitates teacher-principal working relationships. Therefore, if there be one bit of advice that deserves wide acceptance, it is for a principal to cultivate his coaching skills as a means of improving the evaluation process.

Evaluator's Attitudes Toward Evaluation

The performance approach, so radically different from personality rating, presents an entirely new perspective on evaluation. It also presents a significant professional challenge to make it work positively in the educational setting. Centering evaluative efforts upon performance and results, involving those being evaluated in setting organizational objectives and achievement targets for each job, and formalizing the evaluatee-evaluator partnership in performance planning and analysis—all these ideas represent tremendous advances by school districts in the concept of purposeful evaluation. Probably the most significant forward step, however, is the idea that evaluation is a planned, genuine effort to achieve better job understanding and an inner commitment on the part of those doing the work to improve the results of their labors.

School systems are at different stages in developing and conducting effective evaluation procedures. Also, principals vary in their knowledge of and attitude toward evaluation as a part of their leadership responsibilities. The size of the school system is not the paramount question; neither is the existence of well-developed and systematic evaluation procedures. The point is that principals are obliged to make evaluative judgments about teaching effectiveness. The superintendent may want evaluation reports on teachers, a recommendation for the next higher certificate or tenure is called for, or a judgment has to be made as to the relative strengths of teachers in order to assign them for the coming school year. These needs, and others, call for evaluation judgments whether in a big, complex school system or in one that is relatively small and uncomplicated in structure.

The degree to which principals are able to make good evaluation judgments is often regarded as a mark of their competence as leaders. Estimates of teaching competence can be arrived at by hunch or by a carefully planned process of evaluation. But the validity of evaluation judgments is of paramount concern so it is logical that a systematic process of evaluation is preferable to "playing it by ear" and relying solely on intuitive judgment.

The principal's attitude toward evaluation has a great deal to do with the success or failure of the process itself. For that reason, some attention must be given to various aspects of that attitude. Some principals regard evaluation as an unpleasant task added to an already too heavy workload. Others do not believe they have an obligation to help evaluatees improve their performance through evaluation. Still others feel that evaluation by means of performance objectives takes too much time and prefer checklist, rating approaches. Some principals feel insecure about performing the evaluator's role. All of these feelings probably will adversely affect the successful accomplishment of the evaluation process. On the other hand, it is encouraging to note that an increasing number of principals are developing a positive attitude toward evaluation and are accepting it as a necessary and an important administrative responsibility.

Orientation Toward Evaluation

Webster defines orientation, in a psychological framework, as an "awareness of the existing situation, with reference to time, place, and identity of persons." So it is with principals. Each must sense his relationship to the situation in which he finds himself: What kind of staff does he have? Does he see the staff as an entity or as a group of individuals? What are the staff members' differences—in age, experience, and personal qualities? How competent is each staff member? What strengths and liabilities are evident?

In addition to an assessment of the quantitative and qualitative aspects of their staffs, principals must examine their own feelings toward evaluation and how they may be called upon to make appraisal judgments. What attitude will they assume toward evaluation? This probably will depend upon their orientation to the process. Their attitudes may be one of the following:

Amenability about evaluation but lack of experience with it

Interest in the process and a desire to know more about it

Apathy and indifference toward it

Disdain and, to some degree, hostility toward the whole evaluation concept

Each of these attitudes will influence the success of an evaluation program insofar as the principal is concerned. Therefore, the nature of a principal's orientation toward evaluation makes a great deal of difference.

Experience with Evaluation

Principals are rarely completely secure and comfortable in judging the competence of their teachers. They may feign confidence, giving the impression of great certainty. At the opposite extreme, they may be "frozen" by uncertainty, dreading to commit themselves. They may find it very difficult to come to grips with the need to put the evaluation judgments in writing and interpret them to teachers, especially in the case of those teachers whom they consider to be marginal.

Obviously, the above are extreme attitudes, and most principals, it is to be hoped, find themselves somewhere between the two extremes. Experience over a period of time with an evaluation process tends to give principals a feeling of familiarity with it and a sense of security in its use. On the other hand, if a principal has never been an evaluator (in the sense being considered), he often feels uncertain and sometimes apprehensive when he realizes that he will be required to fulfill the role of an evaluator.

It is possible for principals experienced in evaluation to gain deeper insights into how to make evaluation judgments, to gain greater skill in making them, and to seek ways to refine the evaluation process. In all probability, principals just beginning an evaluation program will concentrate upon the more mechanical facets of the problem, seeking to gain know-how and familiarity with procedural matters.

It should be recognized that time is required for the development of an effective evaluation program. The first year of operation often reveals imperfections not only in the process itself but more particularly in the effectiveness of the evaluator. The second year is usually better than the first, the third better than the second, and so on. Experience refines both the process and its implementation.

Little is gained by delaying the institution of evaluation processes until everything is in complete readiness and in a high state of perfection. Adequate preparation is, of course, essential, but the courage to begin is equally necessary. Refinements and improvements will result from experience.

It should not be concluded, however, that evaluation actions should be carried out in a superficial or frivolous manner. Quite to the contrary, a sensitivity to the dynamics of the evaluatee-evaluator relationship is important. Principals must also be prudent in their use of the evaluation process. They must continually weigh the implications of their judgments and consider the effects their judgments will have upon the present and ultimate effectiveness of the teachers.

In essence, principals must be willing to initiate evaluation actions, aware that they will make some mistakes but confident that, as time passes, they can become more and more effectve in their evaluation relationships.

Knowledge of and Skill in Evaluation Procedures

Effectiveness as an evaluator depends, in part, upon the extent to which the principal fully understands the philosophy and procedures of evaluation. It is wise to be as knowledgeable as possible about the specific evaluation procedures in use in the particular school system in question. In addition, general reading in this field of personnel administration is not only useful but essential. It is important for the principal to know and understand the status and history of evaluation in the system, the purposes and objectives of the process, the procedures and mechanics of evaluation, the role and responsibilities of the principal, the relationship of evaluation to general supervision, the expectations of the superintendent and the board of education, and the outcomes expected or desired.

Knowledge of the process is one thing; skill in applying its procedures is equally important. The latter comes more from discerning experience than from trying to follow the well-intended advice of others. There are, however, some useful suggestions and guidelines, which principals may find helpful as they strive to improve their skills as evaluators (see pp. 55–56).

There are, obviously, still other guidelines that will help principals become more skillful evaluators. Principals need not expect perfection as they strive for improvement, but they can hope for greater competence if they are willing to profit by their mistakes and to work for deeper insight and greater understanding of the evaluation process.

Teacher-Principal Relationship

Rapport with teachers is essential if a principal is to achicve maximum results. A teacher needs to feel that the principal genuinely respects him and is interested in him as a person and as a professional colleague. While a peer relationship may not be totally possible or desirable, a rigid superior-subordinate relationship detracts from a good evaluation climate. Best results are obtained when a "climate of confidence" prevails in teacher-principal relationships. It has been said that a mutual acceptance of the fairness of evaluation is more important and vital than the process or mechanics of evaluation.

A greater sense of personal achievement, job fulfillment, and higher morale is likely to prevail when teacher-principal relationships reflect an easy, face-to-face communication, a sharing of decision making and problem solving, and confidence in each other's integrity and motivations.

7

7

Evaluation as an Administrative Tool

Program improvement and especially the qualitative improvement of teaching performance are important responsibilities of the principal. A plan of deliberate action is required to achieve these goals. Simply stated, such achievement involves planning, doing, and reviewing the results.

The ingredients of an action program for improvement are many. Adequate physical facilities, ample equipment and supplies, good instructional materials, books and teaching resources, a sound curriculum, and competent teaching services are the key components. Teaching service is probably the most crucial. One issue principals face is how to help teachers improve their teaching performances. Among the tools at the principals' disposal is the evaluation process. Through it, they are better able to exercise their own skills in personnel administration, utilize the resources of their staffs more effectively, and promote their own administrative self-development.

Expediting the Work of Others

Principals have essential personnel administrative duties and responsibilities to perform. While they may or may not be involved in the employment of the teachers placed in their building, they must orient and induct them. They must assign them to specific grade levels or subjects. Helping teachers understand the individual differences of their students is a part of their responsibility. Expediting their efforts to accomplish the instructional program is a critical part of a principal's job.

103

The ability to assist in making the performance of the school's total program rewarding is another demand upon leadership skills. The evaluation process described in this volume, with its emphasis upon good planning, deliberate achievement of performance objectives, and systematic evaluation of results with appropriate follow-up action, is a tool of effective administration.

In all aspects of administrative leadership is the underlying need of teachers to achieve personal and professional job satisfaction and fulfillment. Good working conditions, fairness and equity in assignments, morale and esprit de corps, job challenge, capitalization upon particular teaching strengths—all of these responsibilities and others compose a significant part of the principal's personnel administration. The principal, as a personnel manager, is also concerned with each teacher's adjustment to the job, clarification of duties and responsibilities, utilization of instructional resources, adjustment to pupil and parent problems, working conditions and frustrations, need for counseling and guidance, and professional growth and improvement.

A principal has many ways available to him to be a good personnel administrator. No two principals will use the same methods, and no one formula can be suggested for carrying out a good personnel program. However, the same approach used in the evaluation of a teacher's performance can be used to provide good administrative leadership of personnel. The following suggestions may be of some help and deserve reiteration.

1. Learn to know the teachers. Their personnel folders usually will yield much valuable information.
2. Assign teachers to a program wherein their strengths will be capitalized upon.
3. Estimate each teacher's professional assets and liabilities.
4. Help teachers develop a plan for improvement: (a) set targets, (b) work for accomplishment, (c) assess results.
5. Be open to complaints.
6. Correct problems that are amenable to correction. Explain why other changes cannot be accomplished.
7. Communicate to each teacher the principal's expectations as well as those of other administrative officials in the school system.

8. Be a counselor and a friend. Give the time necessary and show empathy for a teacher's problems.
9. Reduce barriers to communication and understanding.
10. Expect to fail with some staff members. Give up reluctantly.

Better Staff Utilization

To some degree, principals must deploy their staffs. They are obliged to try to place each teacher in an assignment that will best utilize his instructional strengths. This is an ideal, of course. Perhaps the principal is never quite able to always put the best person in exactly the right assignment. Yet it is a goal worth working toward. Basically, placement, assignment, and transfer are the tools of staff utilization. The distinction made here between placement and assignment is that the former is used to describe where the teacher teaches; the latter, the specific grade or subjects taught.

In the placement of teachers, principals should help see that a teacher's experience, training, and interests are matched with the school that best suits those qualifications. Probationary and beginning teachers should be placed, insofar as possible, where they will have a fair chance to make a good adjustment and develop into superior teachers. They also should be placed where skilled supervision and guidance is most likely to be available.

In assigning teachers it is necessary that their qualifications be the paramount consideration. Teachers should not be given assignments outside their field of preparation. Fairness and equity should be exercised in the allocation of so-called extra duties and assignments.

Changing circumstances may arise that will require the transfer of an employee. There should be specific policies and procedures, in writing, to govern transfers. These regulations should be stated clearly and be made known to all teachers. Transfer requests should be given careful consideration, and the needs of the school system, as well as the wishes of the teacher, should be the prime consideration in approving or disapproving a transfer.

The transfer process should be used as a means of maintaining a proper balance of youth, experience, and specialized competence among the several schools in a school system. Another important guideline for using transferal as an instrument of staff utilization is that the principals and instructional supervisors as well as the teacher should be involved in making the decision.

In all of these decisions for best staff utilization, the great advantages of the performance evaluation process become obvious; it not only has diagnostic value but improves leadership understanding of the staff.

Administrative Self-Development

Principals have a need for self-development in the fulfillment of their jobs, particularly since the demands upon them, in all phases of their leadership role, have been intensified in recent years. The need for competent teachers, the high turnover in staff, pressures that a changing community and world have placed upon the educational program of the schools, and increased complications caused by the weakening of the home and other social institutions in the community are only some of the problems that have intensified the need for a high level of competence on the part of principals.

The relationship of performance evaluation to administrative self-development is closer than may be assumed at first glance. Along with a procedure for assessing the performance of teachers, there is a need for a well-designed plan of administrative and supervisory performance evaluation. (This is discussed at some length in Chapter 4.) The techniques for evaluating the work of a principal are not greatly unlike those for teachers. The emphasis should be on

1. A better understanding of the scope and elements of the principal's job
2. An assessment of areas of performance that need improvement
3. Establishing a realistic number of performance targets upon which to base concentrated effort in a given period of time

4. Working out a sensible plan of action to achieve results in the areas of concentration
5. Seeking help and guidance from people the principal looks to for administrative assistance
6. Gaining new information and knowledge in leadership performance from professional reading and study
7. Making an honest self-analysis of the results achieved
8. Asking superiors to evaluate performance results
9. Being willing to accept constructive criticism and to profit from experience

These are some of the techniques of self-development, but the best route toward improvement is an inner acceptance of the need for improvement and a willingness and determination to develop a plan for its attainment. An inner awareness of the need for self-development is the starting point, and the genuineness of the desire for self-improvement is the key to the success of all that may be designed to bring it about.

Changing Interpersonal Relationships

As the educational structure has become less and less unified—because of divergent interests and pressures among its components—good relationships among teachers and administrators have become more and more eroded. Cohesiveness in interpersonal relationships has decreased sharply. This fact has to be taken into account when speculating on the degree to which personnel evaluation can be a means to build greater cohesiveness in working relationships.

Collective bargaining, frustrating though it may be, represents one important way interpersonal conflict may be dealt with. By recognizing and accepting the legitimacy of competing claims on resources, within specified ground rules, this method of collective decision making offers a way to resolve conflicts within the organization. The alternatives appear to be managerial dominance or alienated power blocs, with pressures increasing so that conflict resolution becomes an escalating preoccupation of administrators' and teachers' organizations. Neither of these alternatives is likely to be acceptable. Employees won't agree to the former; management cannot afford the latter.

There is little likelihood that teachers' organizations will soon choose to change direction and join with administrators and other groups in reuniting all the components of the education profession into a cohesive community. It therefore becomes important that cohesiveness be established at each level—in individual schools and in school systems as a whole.

Characteristics of Cohesiveness

Cohesiveness is more a product than a process, resulting from a combination of qualities and forces. Although organizational structure may affect cohesiveness, it won't guarantee its existence. In fact, different types of structure may produce varying degrees of cohesiveness. In its heyday, autocratic administration often produced a kind of cohesiveness, accounted for by the benevolence of the chief executive and a willingness on the part of the staff to be led.

As paternalism replaced administrative autocracy, cohesiveness often continued because of the inclination of the leader to take "good care" of the welfare needs and concerns of the staff and even, to a limited extent, to share the making of decisions and determinations—although ensuring that managerial prerogatives remained intact. In both autocratic and paternalistic kinds of administration the key to cohesiveness was a willingness on the part of the staff to be led and to remain a "junior partner."

An integrative type of structure (one in which the various components of management—superintendent, top-level assistants, third- and fourth-echelon administrators, and individual-school leaders) moved toward having clearer and better written definitions of interrelated responsibilities. An all-powerful chief executive gradually gave way to administrative team arrangements. Leadership functions became more highly integrated as it became clear that managing large, complex educational organizations could best be done by a team of able administrators with well-defined duties and responsibilities. Linkages between various levels of the organizational structure became more precisely and more clearly established. As educational organizations adapted "scientific" management techniques (often from well-established and competently run business and industrial models), efficiency became the watchword. Cohesiveness existed in this kind of framework, too.

Early in the 1960s a new force entered the picture—collective bargaining. As teachers' organizations changed the thrust of their interests and replaced subservience with militancy, participatory management replaced integrative relationships in school systems. Components of the leadership team began to see their roles in management as a right rather than a privilege granted by an enlightened chief executive. Participation in management became a negotiated matter in large city school systems. (Participatory management, attained either by means of negotiated contracts or voluntary consent of top management, is not the predominate pattern in all school systems. Its incidence is unevenly distributed throughout the country.) Even though cohesiveness can exist in this form of administrative structure, it has to be nurtured.

Five qualities or forces contribute to a high or low degree of cohesiveness regardless of the size of the school system.

1. Program Thrust. This is probably the most significant contributor to cohesiveness. It is the common denominator around which all components of the school or organization can rally to contribute talents, time, and techniques to achieve programs that have been cooperatively determined and are jointly prized as the raison d'être of the organization.

2. Leadership Style. Every educational unit requires executive leadership. At the school level, this important responsibility usually falls upon the shoulders of the principal. In all types of educational organization, executive leadership is an important contributor to cohesiveness.

3. Communication Flow. The third most potent factor contributing to a cohesive organization is communication—downward, upward, and horizontal. Its importance cannot be overemphasized.

4. Sense of Identity. Inasmuch as a school system is composed of different kinds of participants, each needs to feel a sense of identity with the total enterprise and its purpose. Unless there is such a sense, nothing much happens. A leader may exhort, direct, or try to sell staff members on feeling identified with the organization, but it requires more than rhetoric. There must be direct involvement in the establishment of organizational objectives, in program implementation, and in the assessment of outcomes. In this way identity is established, and unless members of the administrative team feel that sense of identity, cohesiveness is likely to be fiction rather than fact.

5. *Quality of Commitment.* Closely associated with a sense of identity is the quality of commitment. In fact, it is a product of the other four qualities or forces. If there is an exciting program, wise and sensitive leadership, a consistent flow of effective communication, and a high incidence of a sense of identity with the organization, it is safe to assume that the degree and quality of commitment to the organization will be high.

Achieving Cohesiveness

Each school system must design its own plan of administrative operations to fit its purposes, personnel, resources, and depth of determination if cohesiveness is to be achieved. No simplistic recipe can be provided. A process that works is ordinarily a good one, but what succeeds in one situation may not in another.

There are some rather obvious, commonsense suggestions that may be helpful, however.

•   Get broad participation in the process of decision making. Doing so, in itself, tends to generate cohesiveness.

•   Design programs that have substance, will engender broad staff involvement and participation, and have promise of successful attainment.

•   Promote intrinsic motivation. It yields the type of dividends that contribute more to cohesiveness than an overreliance upon extrinsic rewards, although they are not unimportant.

•   Don't overlook the potential value of a disciplined organization. A constructive use of "tight ship" management practices may be more widely welcomed than resisted. Permissiveness is not an unmitigated blessing, and an affirmative use of disciplined leadership procedures is not damaging to cohesiveness. Indeed they can contribute to it.

•   "Practice what you preach" is an old cliché, but it is much more than a slogan. It's the essence of credibility.

- • "Put yourself in the other person's shoes" is also a hackneyed admonition, but nonetheless a sound maxim in the exercise of management prerogatives. It is so easily professed and so readily ignored.
- • Periodically check to see if any progress is being made in the quest for cohesiveness. Feedback may call for an alteration of tactics and strategies.
- • Humanize administrative behavior as an antidote to management myopia. It's very easy to believe in your own infallibility, but fatal to cohesiveness.
- • Top-level leaders are well advised to beware of relying too heavily upon the counsel of too few confidants or only "yes" advisers. The insulation of the chief executive from a balanced input of advice—and, it is hoped, constructive criticism—is destructive to cohesiveness.
- • Build cohesiveness gradually. Its development is a slow-growing, complex process. Repeated modest successes build depth and permanence.

These are merely suggestions—easier to proclaim than to produce. They are predicated, however, upon the belief that schools and school systems can create and renew cohesiveness. Without this belief at the outset, the chances of it happening are reduced. If cohesiveness can be increased, it is reasonable to hope that it may be an antidote to a weakening of interpersonal relations caused by power grabs.

Personnel evaluation, conducted in the manner being advocated, can be an administrative tool to supplement the above suggestions. In fact, evaluation, used as a tool for planning and achieving, can do a great deal to build organizational and managerial cohesiveness.

8
Developing or Revising Evaluation Programs

It is impractical, if not impossible, to prescribe a surefire blueprint for designing and implementing an evaluation program to fit every school system. On the contrary, each system must construct its own plan to accommodate any unique requirements. There are some pathways, however, that can be suggested. The challenge is to distinguish between a pathway and a pitfall on the way to an effective evaluation program.

The designers of evaluation procedures are cautioned to keep asking themselves over and over again, at each step, whether the approach being recommended will work. How will those who are affected be brought to understand and accept the program? The workability of a program is a very important consideration, much more so than any planning group's disposition to exercise creativity in establishing an evaluation program.

The Evaluation Planning Committee

There is a better chance of gaining staff acceptance of and commitment to an evaluation program when representatives of all components of the staff—especially those whose personal welfare is affected by the process—have a role in its design, development, and implementation. This means that teachers, administrators, and supervisors must be deeply involved. Students and parents, too, can contribute usefully to the design of a program.

Specifically, central-office specialists, principals, supervisors, and teachers are the prime contributors. Students and parents

Figure 8.1

Planning Committee

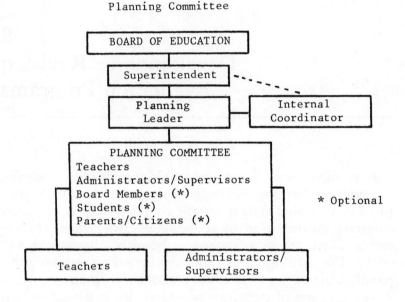

may serve on an evaluation committee as auxiliaries. Some planners would also include representatives of the board of education. As long as the participation of the board's representatives does not outweigh the input of the other participants, there is no reason why they should not serve on the committee.

The justification for a composite committee is rather obvious as each component has a distinct interest in the outcome of the committee's work. Teachers will be evaluated by the process; principals will serve as evaluators as well as being evaluatees; and supervisors may function either as direct evaluators or in consulting roles as determined by the planners. Central-office specialists have expertise to contribute, and client input is an essential element inasmuch as students and parents are the consumers of educational services, the ultimate purpose of an evaluation program.

Committee members are the designers and builders of a specific evaluation process. They will

Formulate a rationale for the procedures

Differentiate between general performance areas and goals and explicit objectives or targets, suggesting techniques for establishing both

Outline ways to correlate day-to-day performance and target attainment

Develop the steps in the evaluation process

Indicate ways to assess target fulfillment and overall performance

Explain the purpose and significance of evaluation conferences

Design appropriate evaluation forms and records

Produce a handbook of procedures incorporating all facets of the evaluation process

Propose concrete ways to institute the program

Recommend in-service activities so that both evaluatees and evaluators will properly understand the procedures

It can be readily seen that the evaluation committee has demanding responsibilities. The quality of its work is critical to the success of the process. To neglect the formation of a strong evaluation committee or to give it scant support is likely to be costly.

The size of the committee will vary. If membership is determined on a proportional basis, it may be a large committee. If so, smaller task forces can and should be formed to carry out specific assignments. A coordinating committee, composed of task-force chairmen, can give general direction to the project.

Some pathways and pitfalls in committee formation and operations are predictable.

PATHWAYS

1. Make the committee a viable organization. See that it is not a rubber stamp mechanism existing only to carry out top administrative wishes or to comply with government regulations.

2. Deliberately seek the understanding, involvement, and support of the teachers' organization. Opposition can be a millstone and can occur despite the fact that perfor-

mance evaluation represents fulfillment of teachers' desires for participation that have been strongly voiced by their spokesmen for years.

3. Budget funds for clerical support and substitute teachers so that committee members will not be obliged to meet only on their own time. After all, performance evaluation actually amounts to a fundamental rearrangement of the complete operation of the school district.

4. Provide feedback reports to the total staff as the committee's work proceeds. This will pay big dividends in achieving staff understanding, which is one of the absolute essentials of any plan.

5. Top administrators should give high priority to the work of the committee and should recognize its accomplishments. Roadblocks in the path of the committee's progress should be removed. Many plans succeed or fail because of this last point.

PITFALLS

1. Overdomination by central-office representatives may result in an accusation of paternalism.

2. Letting the substance of the evaluation process become a negotiable matter at the bargaining table will make evaluation an exercise in futility. The substance of the process should be the product of the evaluation committee.

3. Handpicking members, so as to reflect the top administration's interests and wishes, will make the committee more or less ineffective, if not useless, even when the administration's motives may be flawless.

4. Unrealistic deadlines for completing the committee's work may jeopardize productive outcomes. On the other hand, letting the work of the committee drag out interminably is also a mistake—and has been the tragic fate of too many attempts to set up a performance evaluation program.

5. Inconsistent support or sudden "changes in signals" by top administrators, while the committee is at work, is a recipe for failure. The fundamentals of performance evaluation have been sufficiently tested to assure fair

treatment for teachers, management, and the school board; administrative attempts to manipulate the committee's work are unwarranted and obvious.

Multiplicity of Purposes of Evaluation

It is not uncommon for boards of education and school administrators to insist upon the development of a kind of evaluation program that will simultaneously and conveniently carry out a number of management functions. While it is understandable to want an evaluation program that will serve multiple purposes, it must be recognized that some purposes may be in conflict with each other.

Evaluation to promote improvement and steps to terminate services may sometimes be at cross purposes. Both are necessary but have to be designed and carried out in different ways. A plan of evaluation to stimulate growth and development and one to support differential pay programs are not necessarily compatible. Adaptations have to be made in order to achieve these differing purposes.

If an evaluation program that will serve differing purposes is desired, it is important to show how the procedures adopted are designed to accomplish the diverse purposes.

PATHWAYS

1. State explicitly the purposes the evaluation program is intended to accomplish. When purposes conflict, be sure to admit that particular fact and indicate how the procedures have to be modified to achieve the different purposes.

2. Make provisions for adapting the procedures to identify substandard service and indicate how cases of inadequate performance will be handled.

3. Recognize that evaluation by means of performance objectives is not well suited to instituting or implementing merit pay. Evaluation by objectives is designed primarily to improve performance and not to produce quantitative ratings of sufficient precision to base differentials in pay on them. The determination of merit pay is best made as a management decision. Evaluation data may reinforce the

manager's judgment, but such information is best used only as a supplemental input.

4. Credibility is the key word. When purposes other than the improvement of performance are to be served by the evaluation process, be on the alert. The evaluatees should be fully aware of the fact. To profess one purpose and pursue another, which may be antithetical, undermines confidence and erodes the value of the evaluation process.

PITFALLS

1. Persistence in wanting a multipurpose evaluation plan without recognizing the inherent problems in such an approach complicates development of the plan.

2. Neglecting to make evaluators aware of how to use evaluation procedures to accomplish different purposes can be costly.

3. Failure to use evaluation as a means to improve performance renders it less effective.

4. Overexpectations and unrealistic conceptions as to what evaluation can accomplish as a management tool are disservices to the evaluation process.

5. Slowness in modifying the evaluation procedures when it is evident that modifications are necessary to accomplish specific purposes hampers the effectiveness of the evaluation program.

Responsibility Criteria

Job definition and clarification are basic to effective evaluation. To understand clearly what is expected of one is a prerequisite to the formulation of relevant performance objectives, and responsibility criteria are the yardsticks against which one can measure the extent to which the objectives are achieved.

A criterion is simply the statement of optimum performance of one aspect of the total job. For instance, in the area of instructional competency, a criterion might be individualizing teaching techniques to meet learner needs. The criterion is quite general and merely indicates that effective teaching must adapt to individual needs. Specification is achieved when explicit performance objectives are designed to help increase a teacher's ability to individualize.

PATHWAYS

1. Criteria must be relevant to ongoing performance and cover the entire job.

2. Criteria must be general enough to apply to the total teaching staff. It is not necessary to develop separate criteria for each category of teachers.

3. Criteria are tailored to each category or individual when performance objectives (job targets) are formed.

4. Criteria should be used as bench marks of quality. They are indexes of desired attainment.

5. Criteria should be designed by the evaluation committee and should reflect the best thinking of each component of the committee.

PITFALLS

1. Designing separate criteria for each category of the teaching staff needlessly complicates the evaluation process.

2. Phrasing criteria in vague, ambiguous language confuses both evaluatees and evaluators.

3. Dominance by top administrators in forming criteria is counterproductive.

4. Failure to collect responsibility criteria developed in other school systems and to adapt sound ideas that appear applicable overlooks a useful resource.

5. Failure to design criteria that best fit the requirements of the local school system, generally by copying those of another system, is an unwarranted risk and gamble.

Evaluation Procedures

It is essential that all aspects of the evaluation program be explicitly stated. Topics to be covered should center upon

1. Rationale of philosophy of the evaluation process

2. Categories of evaluatees
3. Frequency of evaluations
4. Designation of evaluators
5. Evaluation procedures
6. Timetable of accomplishment
7. Appeal process
8. Relationship to negotiation (where applicable)
9. Multiple uses of the evaluation process (i.e., improvement, pay, termination, etc.)

PATHWAYS

1. If evaluation procedures are to be applied differently for beginning teachers, experienced teachers new to the system, experienced teachers within the system, or those individuals whose performance is substandard, the differences should be indicated.

2. Those who are to serve as primary and supplementary evaluators should be designated. The role each is to perform should be clearly defined, especially with regard to the collection of performance data.

3. The relationship of the evaluation procedures to the supervisory process should be made clear.

4. The roles of students and parents (if any) in the evaluation process must be well defined.

5. An appeal procedure should be provided for those who may be dissatisfied with their evaluations.

PITFALLS

1. Hastily prepared, poorly conceived, and incomplete evaluation procedures are little better and perhaps worse than none.

2. Complex and involved procedures complicate and tend to defeat, rather than facilitate, the evaluation process.

3. Procedures that put excessive and unrealistic demands upon principals as evaluators are inadvisable.

4. Failure to consider innovative ways to carry out the evaluation process (e.g., collegial procedures) could lessen its effectiveness.

5. Adherence to the once-a-year evaluation cycle for all

evaluatees is unproductive and tends to perpetuate the rating syndrome.

Forms and Records

Paperwork: how much is necessary and what kind? Plan on enough to get the job done but not so much that the evaluation process gets bogged down and flounders under the weight of voluminous forms and involved record keeping. This is the hazard of bureaucracy. Guidelines are easy to prescribe, but each school system must determine how many and what types of forms and records are actually necessary.

PATHWAYS

1. Strive for simplicity. Complicated, involved forms and records confuse more than clarify evaluations. There should be a good reason for each form, and it should be able to be used with a minimum of difficulty. The preoccupation of committees with forms probably has been one of the most serious handicaps to the adoption of performance evaluation plans. Teaching and administrative work are not done by checklists.

2. If multiple copies of forms and records are required, design them so that completing and processing them will not be tedious.

3. Be sure that evaluatees receive copies of all completed forms and records since evaluatees are vitally concerned with the contents. The communication of evaluative results has been incompetently handled in education for generations.

4. Make provision on evaluation forms for evaluatees to dissent from the assessments of the evaluator if there is reason for disagreement. Concurrence is not essential; performance evaluation is a partnership process and must be respected as such.

5. Include some or all of the following items on the evaluation form or forms: (a) statement of specific performance objectives, (b) self-evaluation estimates, (c) assessments of the evaluator, (d) estimate of overall performance,

(e) general comments by both evaluatee and evaluator, (f) signatures of both parties, and (g) date of completion of process.

6. Attach a supplementary summary record that may show the following kind of information: (a) record of contacts, with dates, between evaluatee and evaluator, and nature of assistance and (b) in the case of an evaluatee doing substandard work, the evaluator should summarize help given, strengths, areas needing improvement, and recommendations for further action. This information is mandatory in such instances; in superior plans such a summary is a universal component.

PITFALLS

1. Overreliance upon numerical assessments (i.e., five-point scale ratings) tends to complicate evaluations. The temptation to get involved in a "numbers game" is particularly strong in education.

2. Ambiguous evaluation statements may seem to keep the evaluator out of hot water, but they are self-defeating. They don't give a clear and accurate picture of the situation.

3. Putting innocuous assessments in writing but talking with others in a way that reflects a different (and usually less complimentary) evaluation is destructive. Honesty and forthrightness are essential in performance evaluation.

4. When an evaluatee is performing below a satisfactory level, the failure to document help given and contacts between evaluatee and evaluator puts the latter at a disadvantage if and when due process requires documentation. Obviously, such neglect is also a violation of performance evaluation fundamentals.

5. Carelessness in maintaining confidentiality in evaluation record keeping undermines the climate of confidence that is implicit in the process and is essential to its success.

Further Observations on Evaluation Programs

It is important to understand that there are other definite

pathways and pitfalls, over and above the basic ones enumerated above, in evaluation by objectives. It is necessary to try to avoid the pitfalls and to strive to follow the pathways.

Balance of Objectives

When the balance between the objectives of the school system and those of the individual are in conflict, or the former dominate while the latter are underemphasized, the evaluation process tends to become pressure-laden and difficult to carry out. Performance objectives ought to reflect the needs of both the school system and the individual. The aim should be to attain a realistic blend of the two. To be most useful, the specific objectives must be cooperatively determined and relevant to day-to-day performance.

Clarification of Job Expectations

A clear understanding of job expectations is absolutely essential, but often an awareness of this necessity is lacking or inadequate. More emphasis on job definition is needed, especially when evaluating by objectives. Whether the employer's expectations are in written form (job descriptions, broad areas of performance, characteristics of excellence, standards of quality, etc.) or indicated orally, it is wise to discuss them before establishing specific performance objectives. In other words, needs assessment—the preliminary step in setting up the objectives—depends upon clarification of job expectations. Otherwise, the setting of job targets has questionable meaning.

Generating Competence and Growth

Evaluation, in and of itself, may not generate improved performance or stimulate development. It is more accurate to say that evaluation is a diagnostic process, the chief purpose of which is to identify areas where improvement is needed or to consolidate and enhance existing performance strengths. These purposes are best achieved when the evaluatee and the evaluator both work together in a concentrated effort to determine the specific performance objectives that are most relevant to the evaluatee's needs.

Enhancement of Communication

Frequently communication and understanding between evaluatee and evaluator are impaired. This is self-defeating. Instead of a partnership, the working relationship may be along the lines of the "boss-employee" syndrome. Communication lines may be tenuous; face-to-face contacts may be minimal; understanding may diminish. Evaluation by objectives, on the other hand, requires a high degree of close contact between evaluatee and evaluator. A better understanding of the other's problems, concerns, aspirations, and expectations is essential.

The Motivation Factor

Stimulation and motivation of the evaluatee are basic to the success of the evaluation process. There is some evidence that such motivation is most likely to occur when the evaluatee plays a major role in planning objectives. Day-to-day work planning activities, in which there is a cooperative effort between the evaluatee and the evaluator, promote higher levels of motivation. The quality of the working relationship between the evaluatee and the evaluator is the key to higher motivation.

Evaluation by objectives offers many opportunities for meeting the divergent needs of evaluatees. This approach to evaluation tailors the process to individual needs by stressing

> Greater and more precise understanding of job content and employer expectations
>
> Recognition that some tasks are more important than others, which puts an emphasis upon priorities or putting first things first
>
> The need to set up specific goals and objectives and to avoid formulating fuzzy targets (accomplishment of the latter may be difficult, and accurately estimating the degree of target attainment is usually also not easy)
>
> The need for evaluator and evaluatee to concur on the pertinence of job objectives and to work together for their attainment
>
> Intensive evaluation of performance objectives as well as consideration and assessment of overall performance

The watchword is improved performance. In a nutshell, that is the essence of evaluation by objectives.

Questions and Answers

The following are some of the specific questions and issues that often arise as evaluation procedures are being considered. The answers are provided to help those who may have to respond to such queries.

Q. *When is the right time to develop a new program or revise an existing one?*

A. The right time is when an existing program is found to be obsolete or is no longer regarded as being useful. If no organized program exists and one is desired, obviously it is time to get going.

Q. *How long does it take to develop or revise a program?*

A. Approximately ten planning days is probably a reasonable period.

Q. *Won't attending an out-of-town workshop or a seminar be an effective way to develop a program?*

A. Workshops and seminars serve best to provide information and inspiration. They are not the best way to develop programs because it is difficult for those who participated in them to communicate what was learned to colleagues back home. Few meaningful evaluation programs get developed merely by attending workshops and seminars.

Q. *Is it necessary to obtain assistance from an external consultant?*

A. It is not necessary if there is someone in the school system who has the background and expertise to guide the development of the program. On the other hand, a well-qualified outside consultant may be very helpful by providing guidance needed for the formation of an effective program.

Q. *What skills and qualities must a good planning leader have?*

A. There are several, among which are the following:

> Knowledge about evaluation theory and practices
> Expertise in guiding a planning committee
> Capacity to be a facilitator
> Patience to hear others out
> Ability to translate ambiguity into coherent and under-
>   standable language
> Tolerance for frustration
> Capacity to overcome unforeseen obstacles
> Capacity to move a group toward a concrete outcome
> Be task oriented
> Ability to keep a committee on schedule
> Commitment to providing feedback to all those who
>   will have to accept and support the planning com-
>   mittee's final product

Q. *Will it be expensive to develop an evaluation program?*
A. There will be costs depending upon when planning ses-
    sions are held, composition of the committee, use of an
    external consultant, clerical services, materials, and other
    such items.

Q. *If an external consultant is used, will there be a need for
    someone in the system to work with the consultant?*
A. Yes, an internal coordinator would be needed to handle
    many of the operational details and clerical matters.

Q. *What kind of planning structure is desirable?*
A. Obviously, there is no one structure that will fit every
    situation. Figure 8.1 is one that is practical and opera-
    tionally feasible.

Q. *How should the reporting of planning sessions be made?*
A. Summaries should be prepared after planning sessions and
    distributed to all committee members for their review.

Q. *How will teachers, administrators, and supervisors in
    general be kept informed?*
A. Digests of decisions made in the planning sessions should
    be sent to all staff members to keep them informed about
    progress in the development of the evaluation program.

Q. *Should a handbook of evaluation procedures be developed when the planning sessions are over?*

A. By all means. These handbooks should be readily available to all staff members.

Q. *How should the evaluation program be implemented?*

A. Orientation sessions should be held. Someone in the central office should be designated to head up the operation of the program. Individual consultation should be provided for both evaluatees and evaluators. In-service sessions should be scheduled to equip the evaluators to upgrade their skills in evaluation.

Conclusion

Performance evaluation offers rich opportunities for the improvement of individuals and the outcomes of their efforts. The question is, What will educators do with these opportunities? If advantage is taken of the opportunity to make involvement come alive and to design promising newer approaches to personnel evaluation, education stands to reap many benefits. If the occasion is used merely to retread old, worn-out procedures by patchwork and cosmetic applications, golden opportunities will have been lost. The challenge lies ahead.

9

Evaluation Programs in Action

There is much left to be done after evaluation programs have been developed. Successful operation is frequently jeopardized by sloppy implementation. Too frequently, a statement of procedures is distributed, and evaluatees and evaluators are left to their own devices to understand the procedures and become prepared to fulfill their roles in the process. Implementation in large school systems requires intensive thought and well-designed strategies. Whether large or small, however, school systems should consider carefully the following as implementation tools and techniques: (1) a good handbook of evaluation procedures, (2) an audiovisual program to supplement the handbook, (3) orientation sessions to introduce the program to the staff, (4) in-service meetings in smaller groups, and (5) skill-development sessions.

In addition to making sure that implementation is well done, there may arise some related issues or problems that bear upon the evaluation process. Three of these deserve some comment.

1. Reduction-in-force. Can and should evaluation be used to help decide who should be released when a reduction-in-force (RIFing) becomes necessary?
2. Compensation and evaluation. Is it possible to use the evaluation process to determine differentials in salary?
3. Evaluation and collective bargaining. Are these two processes compatible or incompatible?

Implementation Tools and Techniques

Handbook of Procedures

Decisions of the committee that developed the evaluation procedures should become the contents of the handbook. Typically, the following topics are included.

Preface. This is a general statement explaining the who, what, how, and why of the program. The statement is normally written by the superintendent. This is important because it shows support for the program by the top level of the school system.

Philosophy. This is a statement of principles and beliefs. It is important that the basic premises, upon which the procedures are based, are indicated. The following is a typical excerpt: "inherent in this evaluation process, is the belief that all persons are capable of improvement throughout their professional careers. Opportunities can and should be provided to make this happen. This evaluation program is predicated upon this principle."

Desired Outcomes. This section deals with specific purposes. Included might be the following typical excerpt:

> It is believed that if these procedures are carried out with the care and fidelity with which they were conceived by those who developed them, that those who will be evaluated will increase their effectiveness, improve working relationships with their evaluators, understand better what is expected of them, be more highly motivated to do successful work, become more proficient in planning, doing, and evaluating, and become more committed to the concept of accountability.

Evaluation Model. One way to clarify the evaluation process is to design a graphic presentation of the sequence of the evaluation process (see Figure 1.1). Each step shown in the model will require fuller explanation. This should be done in detail, showing who does what. Role clarification of those who will be involved in the process is vital.

Evaluation Components. This section indicates how the process works, including who evaluates whom; how often; the specific manner in which evaluation is carried out; the roles of the evaluatee, evaluator, and all others who will be involved; a timetable of completion; and ways to resolve differences that may arise between those involved in the process.

Forms and Records. The forms and records that will be used should be included. It is useful to show these in facsimile, if possible. People understand better how a completed form should look if they can see a sample form, filled in as it might be in a real situation.

Substandard Performance. If the outline of procedures includes how substandard performance will be evaluated, this should be covered carefully in the handbook.

Appeal Process. Normally a plan will be provided whereby evaluatees can appeal final assessments they consider inaccurate or unfair. The method for conducting such appeals needs to be explained.

Client Input. If the evaluation process makes provision for client involvement (i.e., students evaluating teachers, teachers evaluating principals, etc.), the way this is to be done needs to be fully explained.

Glossary. A definition of terms used in the evaluation process will be helpful, and it is advisable to provide a glossary.

The initial edition of any handbook probably should be some form that will allow changes and corrections to be easily made, from time to time, as the need arises. This means that printing the initial edition of the handbook is inadvisable. It is highly desirable that the handbook have wide distribution. If it is possible for every teacher and administrator to have a copy, the implementation process will be greatly expedited. At the minimum, several copies should be in each school and office in the school system.

Audiovisual Program

Consideration should be given to developing some form of audiovisual presentation to use in introducing the evaluation program, such as a slide-sound or videotape presentation. The value of such a resource is obvious. It can be used to introduce the process for the first time to the staff as a whole, and it can be used to explain to parent groups how evaluation works. Superintendents can use it for their boards of education and for other groups inside and outside the school system.

If a slide-sound presentation is to be developed, it will usually be designed to run from twelve to fifteen minutes with approximately ninety frames (slides). The best way to develop such a presentation is to formulate idea cards that cover the essential elements of the total evaluation process. These ideas are then put into visual form, pictures and drawings being the most effective ways to do this. The pictures or drawings are then translated into slides, or into video presentations from which slides are made. A taped commentary can be developed that parallels the pictures or drawings.

Depending upon the audiovisual resources of the school system, the cost of this kind of presentation need not be exorbitant. In fact, its cost can be kept within reasonable limits. Since an audiovisual presentation has potential for wide usage, it is a prudent investment.

Initial Orientation

Depending upon the size of the school system, the initial orientation session may be with the total staff. The timing of such a session is very important, however. It should not be scheduled at a time when the agenda is crowded with many different topics. Indeed, it is better to schedule the initial orientation meeting at a time when the evaluation program can be the sole topic.

Two types of orientation sessions are useful. One may be with the total staff so that all will hear the same initial explanation of the program. This systemwide session needs to be followed up with sessions for smaller groups at the school or department level so that give-and-take may occur between the person making the presentation and those who are hearing it. Questions and answers are important for a fuller understanding of the process.

In-Service Meetings

Once the program is in operation, it is necessary to hold, more or less on a continuing basis, in-service meetings to enable both evaluatees and evaluators to deepen their understanding of the process and improve their skills in fulfilling their roles.

It is often assumed that advocacy and exhortation alone are

adequate to bring about changes in evaluation processes, but actually this is very doubtful. A deliberate effort has to be made to bring about change. A desire for change, resources, leadership capability, and effort have to be brought to bear upon the problem. Outside assistance can facilitate such an attempt by guiding the endeavor, but—in the end—change must come from within the organization.

A new orientation toward personnel evaluation is essential. It has to become a positive process, and it must serve able and effective teachers as well as meet the needs of the less successful. The roles of evaluators and evaluatees have to be redesigned. The latter should take more initiative in identifying needs, setting objectives, establishing action plans, attaining the objectives, and. participating in the assessment phase. The evaluator needs to become more of a coach, expediter, motivator, and resource person. This, in the end, in no way lessens the responsibility of the primary evaluator to assess the effectiveness of the evaluatee. However, there should be more collaboration and shared responsibility in carrying out the process.

Evaluation is essentially a planning, achieving, and assessing process. This means a better definition of responsibilities, identification of current needs, the formulation of objectives to meet the needs, designing and carrying out appropriate action plans, assessment of results, and discussing implications of the results. These are the kinds of things that need to be stressed in in-service sessions.

Skill Development

Evaluators have to modify their conceptions about the evaluation process and develop different kinds of skills from those conventionally used when evaluation is basically an inspectional and rating process. Effective evaluation requires close contact between the evaluatee and the evaluator. This develops, on the part of each, a better understanding of the other's problems, concerns, aspirations, and expectations. Communication is fostered, a deeper awareness of common interests is acquired, and a sensitivity to career development needs is awakened.

Another skill to develop is an ability to increase the motivation of the evaluatee. The best chance of this occurring is when the person being evaluated plays a major role in goal setting, which tends to improve the evaluatee-evaluator relationship. Furthermore, day-to-day work planning activities, in which both cooperate, promote higher levels of motivation. The quality of the working relationship between the two is the key to higher motivation.

It is important first to understand the evaluatee's needs and then to assess cooperatively how well these needs can be met within the existing working situation. The needs should be considered in conjunction with the needs of the school system. The highest point of fulfillment is likely to take place when there is a complementary relationship between individual and organizational needs.

Skill development sessions should be, as nearly as possible, "hands on" experiences. Simulations, case situations, taped episodes with critiquing afterward are examples of the types of training techniques that can be used to improve understanding and the skills necessary to carry out the evaluation process.

Issues Related to Evaluation

Reduction-in-Force

Because of decreasing enrollment, many school systems in recent years have been faced with the necessity of reducing the size of their teaching and administrative staffs. In doing so, there has been pressure from teachers' organizations to rely upon seniority as the sole criterion for deciding who goes and who stays, but seniority alone does not guarantee that quality in performance will be retained.

This raises the question of using evaluation results as one of the criteria in making reduction-in-force decisions. Employees usually aren't very enthusiastic about using evaluation data for this purpose because they feel that such information is too imprecise and subjective. Some school systems are seeking ways to so use evaluation data, however, and the following procedures are typical in school systems that have designed a formula to use evaluation data in making RIFing decisions (adapted from the High Point Public Schools RIFing process in North Carolina).

When reorganization, changes in enrollment, program elimination, and/or changes in funding require a reduction in the number of employees, they shall be grouped within their area of certification, classification, and/or assignment and ranked according to the total score on the schedule entitled "Criteria for Establishing Reduction in Staff" (see Form F). Every effort shall be made to reduce through attrition the number of such employees before the reduction in staff procedures are required.

When an employee's services must be terminated due to a reduction in staff, notice shall be provided no less than thirty (30) workdays prior to the end of the employment period. Any career teacher dismissed because of reduction in staff shall have the right to appeal as provided in the tenure (Fair Employment and Dismissal Act) law.

Affected personnel dismissed as a result of reduction in staff shall have a priority on all positions for which they are qualified that become available in the system for the three (3) consecutive years succeeding their dismissal. Their names shall be placed on a list of available employees in order of separation. However, when the High Point Public Schools offer employment in a position appropriate to the dismissed employee's certification or classification and it is refused, then the name of that individual shall be removed from the priority list. To assist separated employees in their employment search, the High Point Public Schools shall provide neighboring school districts with their names, addresses, certification area(s), or classification status.

When grouped for the purpose of staff reduction, teaching personnel holding certification shall be grouped in the following manner:

1. K–3 certification and teaching assignment*
2. 4–9 certification and teaching assignment
3. 7–12 certification and teaching assignment
4. K–12 certification and teaching assignment in areas of physical education, safety and driver education, health education, language arts, reading, music, art, dance, and exceptional children

*Assignment is defined as teaching duties that require at least or more than one-half of the daily schedule.

FORM F

CRITERIA

FOR ESTABLISHING REDUCTION IN STAFF

Name:_____ Date:_____
        Last   First   Middle

Class and Rating: Circle Highest Degree - Bachelor; Master; 6-Yr.; Doctorate

Areas in which certificated: 1. _____ ; 2. _____ ; 3. _____.

Total years taught in this system _____

Total years taught _____

Circle the appropriate descriptor in columns 1, 2, 3, and 4.
Add columns 1, 2, 3, and 4 to compute total score in column 5.

	1	2	3	4	5
Point Value*	Highest Earned Degree and Corresponding Certification	Evaluator's Rating	Years Taught in This System	Total Years Taught Outside This System	Total Score
-0.4		1.5 ⎤ Needs Improvement			
-0.2		1.6			
0		1.7			
0.1	Bachelor's	1.8-1.9 ⎦	1	2-5	
0.2		2.0-2.1 ⎤ Effective	2	6-10	
0.3	Master's	2.2-2.3	3	11-15	
0.4		2.4-2.5	4-7	16-20	
0.5	6th Year	2.6-2.7 ⎦	8-11	21-over	
0.6		2.8 ⎤ Highly Effective	12-16		
0.7	Doctorate	2.9	17-22		
0.8		3.0 ⎦	23-over		
				TOTAL	

Signature of Employee: _____

Signature of Supervisor: _____

* The point value for column 2 (Evaluator's Rating) will be doubled. All
other columns will have the indicated point value. As a result, column 2
will be weighted in relationship to the other three columns.

The first to be grouped and separated shall be personnel who have not met Class A certification requirements; the second, personnel with expired certificates; third, personnel employed for either short-term or temporary positions and who signed an agreement at the time of their employment that their services would no longer be required when these specific positions were terminated; and fourth, all other personnel. For the purpose of staff reduction, classified or other noncertificated personnel shall be grouped by categories of position and the Criteria for Establishing Reduction in Staff shall be applied.

Explanation of Form F

1. Data for Column 2 (on Teacher, Aide, and Administrator Form) will be obtained by assigning points to the assessment categories used in evaluating duties and responsibilities of the persons in question (see Table 9.1 for point values for evaluator ratings).

2. An evaluator's point average will be determined much as a student's grade point average is determined. Such a process is necessary to convert the Summary Evaluation Report and other rating reports into data that can be used for establishing a reduction in staff.

3. When available, the average of the evaluator's point average on the two most recent final evaluations will be used. However, an employee new to High Point or one who was not evaluated during the preceding school year will have only one evaluation available for determining an evaluator point average to be used in Column 2 (for certificated personnel).

Table 9.1

Conversion Tables for Translating Summary Ratings into Point Values

Teachers/Aides		Administrators	
Highly Effective	= 2.8 - 3.0	Highly Effective	= 2.8 - 3.0
Effective	= 2.0 - 2.7	Effective	= 2.0 - 2.7
Needs Improvement	= 1.5 - 1.9	Not Effective	= 1.5 - 1.9

4. The point value for the Evaluator's Rating (Column 2) will be doubled. All other columns will have the indicated point values. As a result, the Evaluator's Rating will be weighted in relationship to the other columns.

5. For determining a year, an individual must have been on the payroll for at least six months of a given school year.

Compensation and Evaluation

A traditional apprehension of teachers is that evaluation will be used, in some manner, to fix salaries. Pressure to find a satisfactory way to rate performance and fix compensation accordingly has persisted over the years. The stumbling block has always been an inability to find a foolproof evaluation process. School systems have tried various forms of merit rating, but the practice has never been successful enough to become widespread. Will not teachers, therefore, resist evaluation in any form and especially use the process of collective negotiation to thwart its adoption?

Paradoxically, collective bargaining may be the very process to accelerate some form of merit pay. The reasoning goes something like the following.

• Collective negotiation has tended to elevate salary levels to the point where the public is beginning to resist paying the increased cost for teaching service unless a deliberate effort is made to work out differentiated pay plans.

• School boards and school administrators will be pressed to develop ways to avoid paying teachers—able, poor, and indifferent—the same salaries based solely on training and experience.

• Teachers' associations and unions will continue to resist attempts to institute so-called merit pay plans.

• Yet some form of evaluation may actually be accepted through negotiation. Not that teachers will promote it, but it may be reluctantly accepted in order to assure further escalations in pay.

It is probably easier to use evaluation data to help determine compensation for administrators and supervisors, although they, too, are not enthusiastic about the prospects of doing so. They, as most teachers, are dubious about the use of conventional methods of evaluation for this purpose. However, some school systems are using evaluation data to help determine compensation for administrative and supervisory personnel. The following describes, in part, the manner in which this may be done (adapted from a plan developed by Community Unit School District 100, Belvidere, Illinois).

While the primary purpose of the administrator evaluation program is to increase the competencies of administrative personnel, an additional outcome is possible; namely, to provide a means to enable an administrator to qualify for an incentive increment.

For example, the basic salary of an administrator is determined by means of an established formula. The incentive increment is not tied to the formula; it is a separate entity. The amount of the incentive increment is determined by means of the administrator evaluation program as explained below:

• The board of education will allocate annually a fixed amount of money over and above that appropriated for basic salaries. This allocation will be used for incentive increments.

• The total amount allocated divided by the number of administrators eligible to qualify for an incentive increment will determine the possible maximum an eligible administrator can earn each year.

• The actual amount of the incentive increment that will be recommended by the superintendent is determined by ratings received as a result of carrying out the provisions of the evaluation program.

• Evaluation ratings will be based upon (a) extent of achievement of objectives (weight, 30 percent) and (b) effectiveness in overall performance (weight, 70 percent).

• The administrator may earn up to 30 percentage points in Part I, Achievement of Objectives, and 70 percentage points in Part II, Effectiveness in Overall Performance.

Part I. Achievement of Objectives (Percentage Points)

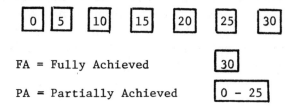

Part II. Effectiveness in Overall Performance (Percentage Points)

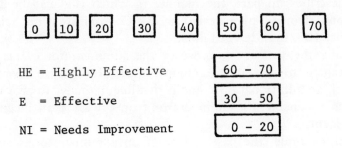

- The sum of the percentage points in Parts I and II will be the multiplier for calculating the actual amount of the incentive increment.

Figure 9.1 shows one way evaluation data can be used to help determine compensation. It must be emphasized that there is, first, a basic salary and the amount calculated using evaluation data is a bonus or incentive increment. Great care must be taken to involve administrators and supervisors in designing any plan to use evaluation data in salary determinations. Such a plan should not be thrust upon them.

Collective Bargaining and Evaluation

It was suggested earlier that, inadvertently, collective bargaining might be the means of achieving some sort of merit pay for teachers—if the point were reached where that was a way to gain increases in pay that otherwise might be difficult to attain. The chances of using collective bargaining to achieve merit pay are not very great.

Employee groups like to use collective bargaining to put constraints on the evaluation process, i.e., to put restrictions on the way employers can evaluate their employees. In other words, if employee groups can get restrictions negotiated and put in the master contract, the freedom of management to design and implement evaluation programs will be limited. To what extent can and should collective bargaining be used to control the development and implementation of evaluation programs for employees? A generalization that responds to this

Figure 9.1
Method to Calculate Increment

$$M_t \times M_i = A_i$$

M_i = Maximum possible amount of increment

M_t = Multiplier (total percentage points)

A_i = Actual amount of incentive increment

Example

Part I	Objectives	Rating	% Points	Average Score
	A	FA	30	
	B	FA	30	
	C	FA	30	
	D	PA	25	
	E	PA	20	
			135 ÷ 5 =	.27

Part II	Area	Rating	% Points	Average Score
	I	E	50	
	II	NI	20	
	III	E	50	
	IV	E	50	
	V	E	40	
	VI	HE	70	
	VII	HE	70	
	VIII	HE	60	
	IX	NI	20	
			430 ÷ 9 =	.477 or .48

Actual incentive increment .27 + .48 = .75 x $1,000 = $750

question is that the evaluation process itself—i.e., the right to assess the quality of teaching performance—should *not* be a negotiable item. In other words, a school system should reserve the right to have an evaluation program for all its employees. Some school systems have already yielded, through negotiation, too much with regard to their prerogatives to evaluate their employees. Once this is done it is very difficult, if not impossible, to retrieve lost prerogatives.

When it comes to the manner in which an evaluation process is to be carried out, there are many reasons why the process itself should be developed cooperatively by teachers, administrators, and supervisors. This calls for "around the table" rather than "across the table" dialogue.

If a program of personnel evaluation is to operate smoothly and effectively, it is advisable that someone reasonably high in the organizational structure of the school system be designated as coordinator. Without a coordinator who is committed to and responsible for a program, an evaluation program may languish and falter for lack of dynamic direction.

Responsibility for the administration of a program may be centered in one of several divisions or offices of the central office. The personnel or staff development departments are frequently given this assignment. The key to success is to be certain that the individual so designated be very familiar with the procedures and dedicated to the program's value and importance.

Finally, the programs should be carefully monitored, both for content and procedural effectiveness. When changes are called for, they should be made, since evaluation is a dynamic process.

10
Using Results of Evaluation

Results of Evaluation

There are several outcomes that can be reasonably expected when the approach to evaluation that is described in this work is used.

Job Clarification

The nature and scope of an evaluatee's job, whether for a teacher or an administrator, often are imprecisely understood. It is frequently assumed that the teacher or administrator knows what the job entails, even though performance expectations may never have been specifically communicated. It is not uncommon for a teacher or an administrator, when learning that his work hasn't measured up to the requirements of the evaluator, to say that no one ever clarified what was expected of him. Furthermore, many evaluatees have a limited concept of the total requirements of their jobs. So one of the most important outcomes of evaluation based on performance objectives is a clearer understanding of what is expected. In other words, a better definition of duties and responsibilities is an important result of this approach to evaluation.

Feedback Utilization

Another important outcome is a better utilization of performance feedback. As the evaluation process yields significant data, the evaluatee is enabled to alter performance strategies, modify objectives, and perfect instructional or administrative procedures. Feedback can be used when it will do the most good and this is a highly positive factor.

Systematic Data Collection

Frequently performance data are gathered sporadically, and judgments are made using insufficient data. The performance objectives approach to evaluation puts a premium upon systematic and careful collection and recording of data. This tends to give great validity to performance assessments. In instances where performance is substandard, systematic data collection is imperative.

More Productive Working Relationships

Evaluation by objectives requires evaluatees and evaluators to work together in seeking to attain productive results. Teachers, principals, supervisors, and department heads have unique roles to play and responsibilities to perform. This interaction can and should generate better working relationships.

Responsiveness to Client Needs

Students and their parents are the clients, the consumers of educational services provided by teachers, principals, and supervisors. While most evaluation procedures minimize the concerns of clients, they make informal, and sometimes critical, evaluations of teaching and administrative performance. The challenge to the architects of evaluation procedures is how to use client input wisely and usefully. Each school system will have to decide for itself if this shall be done and, if so, how. To ignore client interest in performance can be a costly omission.

Affirmative Attitude Toward Evaluation

It is widely believed that evaluation is viewed as a negative process by a very large number of teachers, administrators, and supervisors. Evaluation by objectives—because it stresses growth and improvement as its prime purposes—tends to change a negative attitude into a positive one. While it is unlikely that 100 percent of teachers, administrators, and supervisors will view even this kind of evaluation as an affirmative enterprise, the probabilities of such a change in attitude are much greater than if traditional evaluation procedures are continued.

Documentation of Dimensions of Incompetency

When it becomes necessary to document the dimension of substandard or unsatisfactory service, this type of evaluation can and will yield the kind of information needed to meet the requirements of due process. While this is not the prime purpose of the evaluation process, it is an important secondary purpose.

Increasing Competence

Evaluation, in and of itself, may not increase competence or even stimulate professional growth, especially if the evaluation is basically a postperformance rating without reference to the identification and establishment of performance objectives. Competence may be increased and growth stimulated if change occurs in performance—if that change reflects improvement.

It is more accurate to say that evaluation should be a diagnostic process, the chief purposes of which are to identify areas where improvement is needed or to consolidate existing performance strengths. The process most likely to generate increased competence and to motivate growth is interaction between the evaluatee and the evaluator designed to bring about goal fulfillment. Evaluation tells what needs to be done; supervisory monitoring, assistance, and follow-through produce the growth and development.

The incidence of improvement in performance is likely to be greatest when personal objectives are given as much weight as systemwide goals and the evaluatee functions in a peer relationship with the evaluator. The possibility that these two positive factors will occur is greater in evaluation by objectives than in any other form of assessment.

Using the Results

The evaluation process described in this volume is merely a means to an end. The end, of course, is an improvement in the performance of an individual. In one sense of the word, any evaluation process is merely a technique for "taking a picture" of the status quo at any given time, a device for getting "the facts" that will make it possible to judge what should be done next. A comparison might be made with the work of physicians who are trying to diagnose illnesses and prescribe corrective actions. The physicians may need to make a great many tests and to observe the patient for a period of time in order to collect the necessary data that will enable them to make a judgment as to the nature of the illness and what the therapy should be. While this comparison is an oversimplification, it must not be forgotten that the purpose of the whole evaluation process is to develop a basis for improvement in performance.

Improvement can come about in two ways. First, and perhaps most important, it can be achieved through the efforts of the individuals themselves. To the degree that they become self-enlightened and sensitive to their own strengths and short-comings and begin to see the need for improvement, they will be in an advantageous position to move forward in a program for their own improvement and development. The second way in which improved performance can be achieved is through the leadership, help, guidance, and stimulation that a sensitive evaluator can provide an evaluatee.

The outcomes of evaluation, therefore, will be found in the efforts taken by both the evaluatee and the evaluator to correct what may be considered deficiencies and to consolidate and further develop what may be considered the successes of performance. A good evaluation provides the information needed for further improvement and increased effectiveness.

Summary of Results and Goals

Performance evaluation has many important advantages over conventional rating systems.

1. Long- and short-term objectives of the educational enter-prise can become a more integral part of the evaluation process.
2. The responsibility criteria provide the basis for setting individual performance targets. As a result of thinking through the interrelationships among the various aspects of a job, there is a more effective targeting of individual effort.

3. The outstanding and poor performers receive primary attention, spotlighting those who may be eligible for promotion and those who will require considerable help, additional training, or possibly even termination.
4. Personality plays a much less important role in the final evaluation under the performance concept for the focus is on what the evaluatee does rather than what is thought of him as an individual. Thus, subjective criteria are replaced by objective ones.
5. Performance evaluation tends to require that both parties think hard about educational objectives, particularly long- and short-term targets, and work more diligently for accomplishment of those objectives.
6. The individual responsibilities of the teacher, and of the administrator and supervisor, are brought into sharper focus.
7. Practical work tasks are identified and concentrated upon. These are much more tangible and amenable to action than are the more subjective results of other kinds of evaluation.

Nothing will actually happen in any school system by way of improvement in performance unless each individual does something about it. The basic philosophy of performance evaluation is that each person can do better than he is now doing. Either as an evaluatee or an evaluator, it is necessary to ask the question, "What effect do my activities have on the others around me as I teach or administer?" Insight is paramount to a healthy personality, and a healthy personality is necessary for effective performance.

Both the evaluatee and the evaluator need to feel a sense of personal security. Unless this can be felt as they work together in fulfilling their mutual duties and responsibilities, it is likely that the full measure of effectiveness possible through interpersonal relationships will fall short of maximum achievement. In the teacher-administrator relationship, there must be a nonpunitive quality. There is a need to listen, to let the other person talk and tell how he feels. Each needs to forgo the necessity for self-justification, and each must keep his behavior consistent with professed intentions. Practicing what is preached is as sound in this area as in any other setting.

Sensitivity on the part of the teacher and the administrator to the work situation in which they find themselves is vitally important. As school systems change and grow larger and more complex, problems multiply and life becomes more complicated. Bigness sometimes increases the distance between a teacher and his immediate administrator and supervisor.

A word of caution to the administrator or supervisor is in order. In the long run, decisions made on the basis of intuition are difficult to defend. This approach may get at the symptoms of problems but not at the real causes. An inability to objectively and rationally diagnose the possible causes of a problem is a mark of immaturity. Showing improvement in this skill is evidence of self-development.

Teaching today is a difficult and complex problem. Being the head of a school in an administrative or supervisory capacity is a demanding responsibility. Working in more and more difficult situations calls for a high degree of flexibility. The teacher, as well as the administrator, is obliged to be capable of changing tactics and procedures to fit the varying situations and conditions. The problems vary, and the attack upon them must always adjust to this variance.

The rational process can and should be applied to problem solving in which the teacher and his administrator are jointly involved. Rational people analyze carefully all the aspects of a problem and apply the scientific process in its solution. This is true even when dealing with people whose problems have strong emotional overtones. The goal is to develop the ability and the skill to be objective, to have understanding, and to be patient in working through difficult problems. One must refrain from drawing hasty conclusions or dogmatically deciding what the ultimate answer is before all the evidence is in.

As the teacher and the administrator understand better the larger purposes of the educational enterprise and gain some insight into how it should and does operate and how they fit into the whole process, there is more likelihood that they will have a feeling of personal fulfillment. The teacher needs this;

so do the administrator and the supervisor. When each sees better how his personal fulfillment coincides with the success of the educational enterprise, maximum results can be obtained.

The purpose of this analysis has been to highlight the significance of evaluation on the basis of job performance rather than on the basis of personality analysis. To the degree that the teachers' and the principals' jobs are amenable to evaluation, job performance evaluation becomes feasible. The goal is to create an awareness that each person needs to be more proficient in carrying out his duties and responsibilities. It is hoped that evaluation will arouse a greater interest in and a keener desire for performance improvement and professional growth and development. These things will not happen overnight. But as the significance of job performance evaluation becomes more deeply appreciated, not only by the teacher but also by the administrator, the possibilities for improvement will be greater. What is important is that new insights may be aroused—that self-analysis may take place and that personal commitments to improvement may be made. With this foundation, it is hoped that more effective performance evaluation programs will grow and develop, either where none now exists or in those situations where modification and revision are long overdue.

Appendixes

Appendix A:
Viewpoints of Parents

The purpose of obtaining viewpoints of parents is to get a better understanding of teacher-parent relationships. The information received can be useful in developing objectives to respond to the concerns of parents.

Sending a questionnaire, containing some or all of the following questions, to a sample of parents is one way to obtain this information; getting the data from a parent-teacher group is another. In order to get candid responses, parents should not be asked to sign the completed questionnaires. Getting this type of information is *optional.*

SAMPLE QUESTIONNAIRE FOR PARENTS

1. Are your child's abilities and interests understood by the teacher?
2. Are your child's talents and needs recognized?
3. Is your child working up to his or her ability?
4. Does your child get discouraged when he or she falls behind in daily work?
5. Is your child covering work that you feel should be learned at his or her grade level?
6. Do you frequently have to urge your child to go to school?
7. Has your child developed new interests in school this year?
8. Does your child often misunderstand the teacher's instructions?
9. Does your child think the teacher dominates class discussions?

10. Does your child have a good idea of how well he or she is doing before getting the report card?
11. Can you tell from comments the teacher puts on papers which areas your child may need help in?
12. Does your child know how the teacher expects him or her to behave in school?
13. Do you feel at ease when you visit the school?
14. Do you feel free to call the school when you have a problem or concern about your child's schoolwork?

Appendix B:
Reactions from Students

The purpose of obtaining reactions from students is to get a better perception of how they feel with regard to what goes on in class and to teacher-learner relationships. It is suggested that an effort be made to gather student reactions about learning activities. Some of the responses may be used in developing specific objectives for the year.

Getting reactions from students is *optional*. It is preferable that students not be asked to sign their names to the completed questionnaire. The questions that follow are meant to be illustrative only; also they are structured for students of elementary school age. More mature questions can be developed for older students (see Appendix C).

SAMPLE QUESTIONNAIRE FOR YOUNGER STUDENTS

1. Do you get enough help when you need it?
2. Do you feel the teacher understands you?
3. Are you afraid to ask questions in class?
4. Do you like school?
5. Are you graded fairly?
6. Are you sufficiently encouraged to take part in school activities?
7. Is your schoolwork too hard?
8. Does the teacher involve you enough in planning class activities?
9. Name the thing you dislike most about your class.
10. Name the thing you like most about your class.

Appendix C:
Student Assessment
of Teacher Performance

If teachers wish student reaction to their teaching effectiveness, the following checklist may be used or adapted. Such checklists are usually optional with the teacher. It is obvious that the age of the student will have a bearing upon the usefulness of this checklist.

SAMPLE QUESTIONNAIRE FOR OLDER STUDENTS

Directions to Student. Please rate your teacher on each item. Circle the number that best indicates your view. If the item is not applicable, circle NA.

I. Subject Matter   Low   High

   1. Understands subject . . . . NA   1 2 3 4 5

   2. Makes subject interesting. . . . . NA   1 2 3 4 5

   3. Keeps up to date . . . . NA   1 2 3 4 5

   4. Knows other subjects . . . . NA   1 2 3 4 5

II. Teaching Style

   5. Explains clearly. . . . . NA   1 2 3 4 5

   6. Comes to class well prepared. . . . . . NA   1 2 3 4 5

   7. Asks challenging questions . . . . NA   1 2 3 4 5

   8. Summarizes major points . . . . NA   1 2 3 4 5

   9. Indicates what's important . . . . NA   1 2 3 4 5

  10. Makes clear assignments . . . . NA   1 2 3 4 5

III. Relations with Students in Class		Low				High
11. Encourages class discussion . . . . NA	1	2	3	4	5
12. Lets students state their views . . . . . . NA	1	2	3	4	5
13. Lets students differ with teacher . . . . NA	1	2	3	4	5
14. Helps students who need help . . . . . . NA	1	2	3	4	5

IV. Teacher Attitudes

15. Likes students . . . . NA	1	2	3	4	5
16. Respects students as individuals . . . . NA	1	2	3	4	5
17. Fair to students . . . . NA	1	2	3	4	5
18. Is available to students . . . . NA	1	2	3	4	5

V. Enthusiasm

19. Likes teaching . . . . NA	1	2	3	4	5
20. Enthusiastic . . . . NA	1	2	3	4	5
21. Makes learning exciting . . . . NA	1	2	3	4	5

VI. Student Attitudes Toward Teacher

22. Like teacher . . . . NA	1	2	3	4	5
23. Respect teacher . . . . NA	1	2	3	4	5
24. Speak well of teacher . . . . NA	1	2	3	4	5
25. Cooperate with teacher . . . . NA	1	2	3	4	5

VII. General Evaluation of Teacher (Check)

____ One of the very best

____ Does OK, but not one of the best

____ About average

____ Has lots of weaknesses

____ One of the poorest

Signature not required.

Appendix D:
Evaluation Programs Developed
by School Systems

Since 1975 the author has assisted several school systems in the development of evaluation programs using the approach described in this volume. In each instance, a handbook of procedures was developed to facilitate implementation of the program.

Amarillo, Texas

Guidelines for Developing a Program of Teacher Evaluation for School Systems Affiliated with Education Service Center, Region XVI, Amarillo, Texas.

Andrews, Texas

Handbook of Evaluation Procedures for Teachers. Andrews Independent School District, Andrews, Texas.

Handbook of Evaluation Procedures for Administrators and Supervisors. Andrews Independent School District, Andrews, Texas.

Baltimore, Maryland

Handbook for Educational Administrative Personnel. Division of Elementary and Secondary Schools, Archdiocese of Baltimore, Baltimore, Maryland.

Belvidere, Illinois

Handbook of Evaluation Procedures for Administrators and Supervisors. Community Unit School District 100, Belvidere, Illinois.

Branford, Connecticut

Handbook of Evaluation Procedures for Teachers and Administrators. Branford Public Schools, Branford, Connecticut.

Christiansburg, Virginia

Cooperative Improvement Evaluation Program for Teaching Personnel. Montgomery County Public Schools, Christiansburg, Virginia.

Council Bluffs, Iowa

Procedures, Administrator/Supervisor Evaluation. Council Bluffs Public Schools, Council Bluffs, Iowa.

Fort Thomas, Kentucky

Handbook of Evaluation Procedures for Teachers and Administrators. Fort Thomas City Schools, Fort Thomas, Kentucky.

High Point, North Carolina

Handbook of Administrator Evaluation Procedures. High Point Public Schools, High Point, North Carolina.

Teacher Evaluation Procedures. High Point Public Schools, High Point, North Carolina.

Manassas, Virginia

Teacher Improvement Program. Prince William County Public Schools, Manassas, Virginia.

Mobile, Alabama

Continuous Improvement and Evaluation of Teacher Personnel, Handbook of Procedures, 1978–79 Revision. Mobile County Public Schools, Mobile, Alabama.

Continuous Improvement and Evaluation of Administrative Performance, 1978–79 Revision. Mobile County Public Schools, Mobile, Alabama.

Oakland, California

Evaluation Procedures for Management Personnel. Oakland Unified School District, Oakland, California.

Orlando, Florida

Evaluation Procedures for Management Personnel. Orange County Public Schools, Orlando, Florida.

Handbook of Assessment Procedures for Teaching Personnel. Orange County Public Schools, Orlando, Florida.

Tinley Park, Illinois

Handbook of Evaluation Procedures. School District No. 146, Tinley Park, Illinois.

Topeka, Kansas

Administrator Appraisal Plan. Unified School District No. 501, Topeka, Kansas.

Warren, Ohio

Systems Approach for Educational Accountability. Warren City Schools, Warren, Ohio.

Selected Annotated Bibliography

Anderson, L. W. "More About Teacher Evaluation." *OCLEA* 5 (1975): 3–6.

> Discusses constraints that impede the adoption of effective teacher evaluation programs and recommends use of a management-by-objectives approach to overcome these obstacles.

Barraclough, Terry. *Evaluation of School Administrators.* Arlington, Virginia: National Association of Elementary School Principals, 1974.

> Covers the literature on evaluation philosophies and instruments, both in theory and practice.

Bolton, Dale L. *Selection and Evaluation of Teachers.* Berkeley, California: McCutchan Publishing Company, 1973.

> Analyzes the processes for selecting and evaluating teachers, showing how the two interact and impact on learning.

_____. *Teacher Evaluation.* Washington, D.C.: U.S. Department of Health, Education, and Welfare/Office of Education, National Center for Educational Communication, 1972.

> Makes the point that teachers and administrators should recognize that the question is not whether teachers should be evaluated, but how systematic the process should be in order to be most effective.

Booth, Ronald R., and Glaub, Gerald R. *Planned Appraisal of the Superintendent.* Springfield, Illinois: Illinois Association of School Boards, 1978.

> Describes principles and procedures for evaluating the performance of the superintendent.

Castetter, William B., and Heisler, Richard S. *Appraising and Improving the Performance of School Administrative Personnel.* Philadelphia, Pennsylvania: Center for Field Studies, University of Pennsylvania, Graduate School of Education, 1979.

Makes a strong case for performance appraisal as an essential function of any organization.

Eckard, Pamela J., and McElhinney, James H. "Teacher Evaluation and Educational Accountability." *Educational Leadership* 34, 8 (1977):613–618.

Stresses the importance of improving teacher evaluation and educational accountability; outlines a model for effective teacher supervision and evaluation.

Educational Research Service Report. *Evaluating Administrative Performance.* Arlington, Virginia: Educational Research Service, 1974.

Examines ways in which administrative personnel are evaluated from three points of view: (a) purpose and process of staff evaluation in education and industry, (b) actions of state legislatures and educational agencies, and (c) the use of administrative evaluation systems and instruments used in selected local school systems.

_____. *Evaluating Superintendents and School Boards.* Arlington, Virginia: Educational Research Service, 1976.

Summarizes current efforts and thinking both of professionals and of lay citizens regarding the best ways to evaluate the performance of superintendents and to assess the effectiveness of operational procedures of local boards of education.

_____. *Evaluating Teacher Performance.* Arlington, Virginia: Educational Research Service, 1978.

Describes current practices of evaluating the performance of teachers in school systems of the United States, including a review of the literature on evaluation. Gives examples of forms and procedures, indicates uses of evaluation results, and includes examples of materials that can be useful to those interested in personnel evaluation.

_____. *Negotiating the Teacher Evaluation Issue.* Arlington, Virginia: Educational Research Service, 1979.

Explores the extent to which the evaluation of teaching performance has become a bargaining issue at the negotiating table. Includes summaries of views of both teachers and management on the subject. Analyzes provisions in recently negotiated master contracts. Reports cases that have been decided by arbitration and public relations boards and courts. Provides samples of contract clauses regarding teacher evaluation.

Farnsworth, Alton U. "Administrator Assessment: A Must for School Boards." *Catalyst for Change* 5, 3 (Spring 1976):18-20.

Suggests guidelines for school boards to follow in evaluating the performance of the superintendent and presents a sample assessment for evaluating administrative personnel.

Glasman, Naftaly S. "A Proposed Structure for Evaluating Personnel for Decision-Making." *Studies in Educational Evaluation* 3, 1 (Spring 1977): 47-56.

Describes a structure for the evaluation of all levels of educational personnel. Establishes six assumptions underlying the rationale of the structure for evaluation.

Greene, Robert E. *Administrative Appraisal: A Step to Improved Leadership.* Reston, Virginia: National Association of Secondary School Principals, 1972.

Designed to help principals participate in the process of developing a new or revising an existing evaluation program. Makes significant suggestions for constructing meaningful systems.

Hansen, J. Merrell. "The Evaluation of Teaching: No Guppies or Goldfish in My Classroom." *NASSP Bulletin* 62, 411 (1978):11-15.

Indicates that evaluation of teachers should be implemented as a meaningful way to improve instruction and that the evaluation criteria must be carefully defined and measured so as to eliminate ambiguity.

Hautala, Lynda W. "An Instrument for Describing Classroom Practices During Reading Instruction." *Reading World* 17, 2 (1977):141-145.

Describes the "Teacher Observation/Interview Guide," which was designed to aid consultants, administrators, and teachers in observing and weighing objectively actual classroom practices in the major areas of diagnosis and instruction.

Hyman, Ronald T. *School Administrators' Handbook of Teacher Supervision and Evaluation Methods.* Englewood Cliffs, New Jersey: Prentice-Hall, Professional Books Division, 1975.

> Details methods, strategies, and forms for implementing a more effective supervision and evaluation program for teachers. Gives guidance on conducting classroom observation, how to use feedback, effective communication techniques, helping teachers with strategies of teaching and the writing of performance objectives.

Lewis, James. *Appraising Teacher Performance.* West Nyack, New York: Parker Publishing Co., 1973.

> Provides step-by-step plans, techniques, and suggestions required to implement a program of school management by objectives, including a way to evaluate teaching performance.

Mallery, David. *Strengths of a Good School Faculty: Notes on Evaluation, Growth, and Professional Partnership of Teachers.* Boston, Massachusetts: National Association of Independent Schools, 1975.

> Outlines steps toward good evaluation: establishing evaluative criteria, exploring the range of evaluative instruments, strategies, and approaches, and student evaluation of the faculty. Advocates a commitment to explore the strengths of the school and individual teachers and the willingness of a group to develop the evaluation process.

Miller, William C. "Unobtrusive Measures Can Help in Assessing Growth." *Educational Leadership* 35, 4 (1978):264–269.

> Makes the point that there are many sources of information about schools besides standardized tests and questionnaires; emphasizes the value of careful, unobtrusive observations that are well focused and intelligently interpreted.

Morse, H. Ogden. "Whom Shall We Fire?" *NASSP Bulletin* 61, 406 (1977):76–78.

> Takes the position that when it is necessary to reduce the size of the teaching staff, nontenured staff members should not always be the ones to be released. Presents criteria for administrators to use in deciding which teachers to terminate.

Olds, Robert. *Administrative and Supervisory Evaluation.* Arlington, Virginia: American Association of School Administrators, 1977.

Gives guidance for professional growth and development of members of the school management team through performance planning, analysis of results, and follow-through.

_____. *Self-Evaluation for Teachers and Administrators.* Westerville, Ohio: School Management Institute, 1973.

Treats self-evaluation not only as a means of self-improvement, but also as an important component in the performance evaluation process. Argues for self-evaluation as a vehicle for creative individual involvement in the planning and evaluation aspects of the total process in quest of a higher level of performance.

Redfern, George B. *Evaluating Teachers and Administrators: Putting the Pieces Together.* Westerville, Ohio: School Management Institute, 1978.

Guides school systems in the initiation of new evaluation programs or in the revision of existing ones. Essentially a how-to book with concrete suggestions for completing the total process.

_____. *How to Evaluate Teaching: A Performance Objectives Approach.* Westerville, Ohio: School Management Institute, 1972.

An earlier version of the present volume.

Robinson, John J. "The Observation Report—A Help or a Nuisance? " *NASSP Bulletin* 62, 416 (1978):22–26.

Surveys Connecticut high-school teachers and their supervisors (principals and department heads) to reveal different conceptions of the value of observation reports.

Sharken, William W., and Tremba, Edward A. "Strategies to Improve Instruction." *NASSP Bulletin* 62, 416 (1978):27–30.

Makes a case for the need for school boards and teachers to begin a serious in-depth interchange about the roles of in-service training and evaluation of teachers to increase pupil learning in the classroom.

Walberg, Herbert J. *Evaluating Educational Performance.* Berkeley, California: McCutchan Publishing Company, 1974.

A source book of methods, instruments, and examples for evaluating educational performance.

_____. "Where They Not Only Evaluate Teachers, They Actually Help the Good Ones and Get Rid of the Bad Ones." *American School Board Journal* 163, 10 (1976):19–21.

Describes a teacher "remediation" plan created by one superintendent and the local teacher organization.